THE TALENTED ONES

Yussef El Guindi

BROADWAY PLAY PUBLISHING INC
New York
www.broadwayplaypub.com
info@broadwayplaypub.com

THE TALENTED ONES
© Copyright 2018 Yussef El Guindi

Cover art courtesy of Artists Repertory Theatre
First edition: June 2018
I S B N: 978-0-88145-781-0

Book design: Marie Donovan
Page make-up: Adobe InDesign
Typeface: Palatino

DEDICATION

To Dámaso Rodríguez, Risa Brainin, Jane Unger and
Luan Schooler: thank you for all your support.

THE TALENTED ONES was commissioned for Table/ Room/Stage, Artists Repertory Theatre's New Play Development Program in 2015.

THE TALENTED ONES was developed through a LAUNCH PAD preview production at the University of California, Santa Barbara—Department of Theater and Dance in 2015. The cast and creative contributors were:

CINDY .... Emily Newsome
OMAR ....Roberto Tolentino
PATRICK...James Reisner
YOUNG OMAR / OMAR'S FATHER........Rigoberto Sanchez
YOUNG CINDY / DANCER CINDY . Joré Aaron-Broughton

Director .... Risa Brainin
Scenic designer..Greg Mitchel
Costume designer..Ann Bruice
Lighting designer .... Michael Klaers
Composer / sound designer .... Randy Tico
Choreographer .... Christina McCarthy
Assistant director...................................Manuel Sherbakoff
Stage manager..Sian Harden
Fight choreographer ....Jeff Mills
Dramaturg .... Ahmed Asi

THE TALENTED ONES was produced at Artists Repertory Theatre (Dámaso Rodríguez, Artistic Director; Sarah Horton, Managing Director), opening on 29 April 2017. The cast and creative contributors were:

CINDY .... Khanh Doan
OMAR ....John San Nicolas
PATRICK .... Heath Koerschgen
YOUNG OMAR / OMAR'S FATHER.............. Michél Castillo
YOUNG CINDY / DANCER CINDY ....Madeleine Tran

Director ....Jane Unger
Dramaturg .... Luan Schooler
Scenic designer ....Daniel Meeker
Costume designer .... Darrin J Pufall
Lighting designer ....Kristeen Willis Crosser
Composer/ Sound designer .... Rodolfo Ortega
Choreographer ....Sarah Jane Hardy
Fight choreographer ....Jonathan Cole
Stage manager ....Michelle Jazuk

CHARACTERS & SETTING

5 actors needed

CINDY, *age range: anywhere from early to late 30s*
OMAR, *from early to late 30s*
PATRICK, *from early to late 30s*
DANCER CINDY, *early 20s*
OMAR'S FATHER, *mid to late 30s*
YOUNGER CINDY, *early 20s*
YOUNGER OMAR, *early 20s*
TRISHA, *mid to late 20s*

CINDY *and* OMAR—*and by extension,* DANCER CINDY, OMAR'S FATHER *and their younger selves—can be of any ethnicity (Though given the dynamics, and what is said in the play, it is more than implied that they are people of color.)*

One actor plays TRISHA, DANCER CINDY, *and* YOUNGER CINDY.

One actor plays OMAR'S FATHER, OMAR *in the club, and* YOUNGER OMAR.

CINDY *and* OMAR's *home.*

Time: The present

ACT ONE

(CINDY *and* PATRICK *are in the kitchen. The kitchen and the living room are connected. She is making a salad, cutting up tomatoes, cucumbers, celery, etc. There's a beer on the table next to her. He is nearby also drinking a beer.*)

PATRICK: I didn't know you wanted to be a dancer.

CINDY: I did.

PATRICK: You never mentioned it before.

CINDY: It never came up.

PATRICK: Was this something you like, seriously wanted?

CINDY: It's what I hoped I would be. It's all I thought about at one time.

PATRICK: Huh. —People usually talk about the things that get their juices going. I can see you doing it.

CINDY: And I don't mean strip dancing, either.

PATRICK: I can see you doing that too.

(CINDY *smiles.*)

PATRICK: I'd be ready with the dollar bills.

CINDY: That I can see you doing.

PATRICK: Cindy in the house. Shaking it up.

CINDY: My old dance teacher said I could have a career, if I wanted it.

PATRICK: You didn't go for it?

CINDY: I still think I will, sometimes.

PATRICK: Oh yeah? You going to classes?

CINDY: Not yet. —I do most of my dancing up here now. *(Taps her head)* I'm tearing up the floor in there. At work; shoving needles into veins. I'm feeling my body execute all kind of dance moves.

PATRICK: Are you jumping back into it?

CINDY: I don't have the time. Or the body for that matter.

PATRICK: I would disagree with that. I would strongly disagree with that assessment.

CINDY: *(She smiles, acknowledging the compliment.)* And it's not like riding a bicycle. You can't just pick it up after years of not doing it. It's more like playing the violin. You work at it everyday.

PATRICK: So? *(As in "do it")*

CINDY: I can be making dinner like now, and where I really am—it's like there's another me shadowing my movements. But the moves are like choreographed. And beautiful. And lately, this other me? This dancer? She feels more real than the daily me doing all my boring routine stuff. The other day, the doctor was giving instructions on a patient and I was miles away.

PATRICK: So, do something about it.

CINDY: Well I can't, can I. You of all people know how much Omar brings in. We do have something called a mortgage. We can't all be pursuing our dreams.

PATRICK: Sure you can. Especially if it's distracting you at work.

CINDY: I know, follow your bliss. But your bliss can be as useful as a heroin addiction. Do you eat celery?

(CINDY *holds up a stalk.*)

PATRICK: No. You know what, go ahead.

CINDY: If you don't like it.

PATRICK: Can I try it first? It's been a while since I've eaten celery.

(CINDY *gives* PATRICK *the celery stalk; he takes a bite. He chews and considers the taste.*)

CINDY: Yucky?

PATRICK: Um—let me keep eating it and see if it grows on me.

CINDY: Don't force yourself.

PATRICK: I'm trying to move out of my comfort zone this year.

CINDY: Another beer?

PATRICK: I'll get it.

(PATRICK *gets a beer from the fridge as he looks at* CINDY *from behind. She feels him looking.*)

PATRICK: I can really see you dancing, now that you say it. You have a great body for it.

CINDY: Most dance instructors would consider me fat.

PATRICK: "Fat"? Some people don't know what they're looking at.

CINDY: *(Smiles)* Thank you. You look like you work out yourself.

PATRICK: I like to watch my figure. The job keeps the calories off, even if I'm on the management side now. You want to show off some dance moves for me?

CINDY: I don't know why I'm telling you this. I can't even make dinner without thinking about it.

PATRICK: I've known you for almost like two years and this is the first time you've said anything.

CINDY: I haven't thought about it this much for months. Before I'd just think "I don't have time". Now it's like—if people have a muse, you know, a guardian angel? Mine is becoming like this psycho, drill sergeant in my head.

PATRICK: Well, shit, that's telling you something.

CINDY: When it can also tell me how to make more money I'll listen. I'm sick of this "just-go-for-it" B S. Like every obstacle can be magically overcome. No, it can't. If my days are packed as it is, if I come home to find nothing's ever taken care of…. I'm sounding like a bitch, and I told myself I'd never go there.

PATRICK: You don't sound like a bitch. I've known a few in my time and trust me, you don't sound like one. Have you talked about this with Omar?

(CINDY *shakes her head.*)

PATRICK: Why not?

CINDY: Because.

PATRICK: He's your husband.

CINDY: *(First word under her breath; somewhat sarcastic:)* Husband. You know—I'm just ticked off enough where I might say the wrong thing so let me just—. And yes, I know at the end of day it's about "personal initiative", as my life coach keeps telling me. God bless "personal initiative".

PATRICK: You're seeing a life coach?

CINDY: I get a discount at the hospital. She councils mental patients and moonlights as a life coach. I was desperate.

PATRICK: What did she say?

CINDY: What everyone says, "just do it". These motivational speeches drive me nuts sometimes.

Alright, the end. I'm tired of hearing myself whine, even if you aren't.

PATRICK: You're not whining, we're just talking.

CINDY: It's become like this continuous—hum, in my head, this thing about dancing.

PATRICK: All the more reason to let it out.

CINDY: I can't just let it out and do nothing about it or I'll scream.

PATRICK: So scream.

CINDY: No, I will fucking scream.

(CINDY *stabs the knife into the chopping board. This is accompanied with a piercing sound, or some dramatic sound cue, and light change. Cindy winces like she's experiencing a sudden and painful migraine. The space behind the kitchen/ living room wall is illuminated, allowing us to view the space and see* DANCER CINDY *already there. Her movements are graceful but not mannered. She moves quickly towards the wall.*)

PATRICK: Cindy? …Cindy?

DANCER CINDY: Cindy.

CINDY: *(To no one in particular)* I can't do this anymore.

PATRICK: Are you okay?

DANCER CINDY: Cindy.

CINDY: I can't keep doing this.

PATRICK: What?

CINDY: Stop. —Stop.

(*Lights fade out on space behind the wall.* DANCER CINDY *is blocked from view as the kitchen/living room wall becomes solid again.* PATRICK *goes to her.*)

PATRICK: Cindy? …You want to sit down?

(The sound stops. Lights back to normal. CINDY *looks disoriented.)*

PATRICK: Dinner can wait, come on. *(He takes the knife from her.)* Let's sit down for a minute.

*(*PATRICK *leads* CINDY *to the living room couch.)*

CINDY: I'm sorry. I get these migraines.

PATRICK: Do you take anything for them?

CINDY: I just need to close my eyes for a minute. *(Starts to rise from the couch.)* A cold wash cloth helps.

PATRICK: I'll get it. *(He moves into the bathroom.)*

CINDY: You're not here to look after me.

PATRICK: *(Off-stage, if the bathroom is not visible)* Stress. If you don't pay attention to it, it will bite you back hard. You need to let go of all the shit you can't control. *(He enters with a washcloth.)*

CINDY: That just leaves all the shit I can control. Which is what stresses me out.

PATRICK: Omar needs to carry his share. *(He puts the folded washcloth on her forehead.)* I don't care if he's going to write the next big novel. He needs to step up and handle his end of things. So you can do the things you want as well.

CINDY: Thanks. That feels good.

PATRICK: I'm serious: if Omar loves you, he has to stop what he's doing and pay attention here.

CINDY: I'm not going back to it. Dancing is a nice daydream. We're all allowed one of those.

PATRICK: That's the problem right there. You've put your dream in the it's-not-possible box. Responsible you says it can't be done because of house payments.

CINDY: House payments aren't a wish. The bank doesn't wish you would pay and if you don't thinks,

"Well, we'll let them keep the house anyway." What's almost as bad as the migraines is this fairy tale that we can all achieve what we want.

PATRICK: It's kind of sad hearing you say that. You're doing everything you can to support Omar, but how practical is what he's doing?

CINDY: He's devoted to what he does in ways I can't be.

PATRICK: Does he even know dancing is this thing for you? He's never mentioned it to me.

CINDY: I've told him. It was one of the first conversations we had. Right after we first met. *(Half to herself)* That already feels like a life-time ago.

PATRICK: But does he know you're still serious about it?

CINDY: I'm not going to dump this on him now.

PATRICK: Were you good at what you did?

CINDY: I was told I was.

(With a light change, the kitchen wall becomes see-through again. DANCER CINDY is seen engaging in a graceful dance—perhaps accompanied by music, or some sort of sound. CINDY, with her arms, sketches in a few of the moves DANCER CINDY is making. Her arm movements will mirror the dancer's.)

CINDY: The other dancers in class would applaud. It's a whole other world to feel your body come alive like that. I'm busy at work all day, and yet I might as well not be in my body. I don't know how I can be so asleep in my own flesh. But when I dance, it's like a whole other me is switched on. Like all the reasons to be alive are in those movements.

(CINDY and DANCER CINDY continue their dance for another beat before CINDY stops.)

PATRICK: Just hearing you talk about it…I bet you could have a career doing it.

(DANCER CINDY *stops dancing and listens.*)

CINDY: Listen to you. The guy who pops a beer and talks sports.

PATRICK: I'm pretty sensitive when you get to know me. I've been known to doodle pictures of unicorns at work.

CINDY: Unicorns, huh?

(DANCER CINDY *approaches the wall. She listens in.*)

CINDY: I guess I wouldn't be telling you this if I thought you'd laugh at me.

PATRICK: I'd never do that. —I've always…I've always really liked you Cindy. Not just because you're my buddy's wife. I know I joke around, and I'm sorry about last Sunday, by the way, when you walked in on us. I know it must have sounded crude, the way we talked.

CINDY: I understand guys like discussing tits and ass. And strippers.

PATRICK: But what I'm saying is, that's not me. I actually have like a keen eye and notice shit. And what I've always admired about you is how much you give of yourself to others. Like my mom. —You're a lot sexier than my mom. But you're the same in the way you sacrifice yourself for other people. I used to get so mad at her for not standing up for herself. Her heart was like this big—top-of-the-line Ferrari engine. But it wasn't taking her anywhere, because she was too busy helping other people.

CINDY: That's a life goal too, helping others.

PATRICK: Well you know what, I want to be helpful too. I want to pay-it-forward, for all the good things people did for me. I would've stayed in prison for all the dumb shit I did as a kid if it weren't for others helping me out. I know it's not my place to stick my nose in, and maybe all I'll do is let Omar know we talked about this.

CINDY: Don't. He'll get upset I shared something so personal.

PATRICK: He has to get a clue at least. It's a sin to walk away from something you love.

CINDY: After he finishes what he's working on.

PATRICK: Why can't you both do what you love? *(Answering his own question)* House payments, house payments.

CINDY: I didn't mean to lay this all on you. It isn't helping my migraine.

(The lights fade out on DANCER CINDY. *The kitchen wall looks solid again.)*

PATRICK: Do you take anything else for it?

CINDY: I just have to ride it out. *(Fondly remembering)* My mom used to kiss my forehead. Like she was sucking the headache right out. That's what she would tell me. Somehow, it used to work.

(On impulse, PATRICK *removes the washcloth, if it's still on, and kisses* CINDY *on the forehead. He lets his lips rest there for a while. She is surprised by the move. He stops kissing. Small beat)*

PATRICK: Was that—was that awkward?

CINDY: No.

PATRICK: Did it work?

CINDY: *(Takes stock of how she feels)* A little…I think it did, yeah.

(PATRICK *thinks a moment, then moves in to kiss her forehead again.* CINDY *stops him.*)

CINDY: A second time would be awkward. —Since we're confessing dreams, what's yours? What do you dream about?

PATRICK: Oh, I have real simple ones. You know: a house, a wife, kids. Three to four kids. Two cars. I don't need a huge patio, but a backyard pool would be nice.

CINDY: The works, huh.

PATRICK: The way I see everyone fucking up around me, not getting even the basics right, doing the ordinary things right seems like the toughest goal. When it comes to doing ordinary shit, I want to be the expert. The go-to guy.

(*A laugh from* CINDY.)

PATRICK: I might even have my own T V show: *Ordinary Shit Done Right, with Patrick Mitchell.* —That's not as sexy as wanting to be a famous novelist.

CINDY: That's plenty sexy to me. It's real.

(CINDY *and* PATRICK *both look at each other. There's a pleasant tension—a sexual tension, even—between them.*)

PATRICK: Given where I started, that is aiming high.

CINDY: That's why it's sexy.

(*Small beat*)

PATRICK: Omar's a good man.

CINDY: I know…I love him.

(*For a moment, that pleasant, sexual tension seems to spike. Small beat*)

PATRICK: Is he late coming home like this most days?

CINDY: You would know. Doesn't he tell you he goes to some coffee place to write after he gets off work?

PATRICK: *(Evasive)* Yeah…yeah he does.

CINDY: *(Seeing that he's keeping something from her)* What? —You have that look. Like you're keeping something from me.

PATRICK: Nah. *(Shakes his head)* no.

CINDY: What?

PATRICK: He, er…I guess he hasn't mentioned anything?

CINDY: About what?

PATRICK: I don't know that it's my, um—place to…

CINDY: Your place to what?

PATRICK: To, er—tell you about his… *(Hesitates)* About his getting fired?

CINDY: Fired? —From work?

PATRICK: He—yeah. That would be the place he'd be fired from.

CINDY: When?

PATRICK: Three—three weeks ago?

CINDY: Fired?

PATRICK: Kinda, yeah. Not "kinda". He doesn't work at the moving company anymore.

(CINDY's up now, if not before.)

PATRICK: Now I feel like a complete snitch.

CINDY: You knew and you didn't tell me?

PATRICK: It wasn't for me to say.

CINDY: Where is he now, Rick?

PATRICK: You know what, I think I should shut up.

CINDY: Rick, where the fuck is he? He's been leaving every morning at the same time like he's going to work.

PATRICK: I don't know. Maybe he's writing.

CINDY: *(Starts dialing her cell phone)* And I bought his check-is-late line. He said you guys were doing some in-house audit and that's why it was late. You should have told me.

PATRICK: No, he should have.

CINDY: The house is going to fall on our heads and we're talking about my stupid dancing. *(Takes a breath; into the phone)* Omar, call me. Rick's here and we're waiting for you. Could you come home right away. *(She hangs up.)* Why'd he lose his job?

PATRICK: I didn't fire him.

CINDY: What did he do?

PATRICK: I went to bat for him. Lots of times. But he kept goofing off. Seriously flaking. One time, listen to this, one time he made himself right at home in the house we were hauling stuff into. Sitting on furniture he was supposed to be moving so he could write. The owner came in and found Omar writing at his desk. The desk he'd just moved into this guy's house. And what did Omar do when he saw the owner? He gives him this really evil look, like what the fuck are you doing interrupting my work? That's nuts, right? We all admire him for his talents, but that's crazy shit.

CINDY: Really? —If he's that focused, he must be close to finishing something.

PATRICK: That's not the point, Cindy. Dereliction of duty and nutty behavior, that's the point.

CINDY: *(Half to herself)* I wonder if he'll really pull it off this time.

PATRICK: Wow. I want a supportive wife like you, if that's all you have to say.

CINDY: He hasn't finished anything for a while. This is good. It's also a complete disaster, but— *(Half to herself)* Shit. I'll—I'll have to find another job on the weekends until he's done.

PATRICK: Are you kidding me?

CINDY: Well he can't stop now, can he, or it'll all be for nothing.

PATRICK: You know, seeing it up close as an adult, what did I know as a kid. You get off on it, like my mom. It's like self-sacrifice is this thing.

CINDY: No, it's like marriage is this "thing". In marriage you give and take.

(PATRICK shakes his head and gets another beer.)

CINDY: I know it may be hard to understand—

PATRICK: It's none of my business.

CINDY: —but he has to make this work. I know he walks around with this—it's not exactly a responsibility. I have it too, in a different way. My family expected other things from me. But with Omar…

(Music cue, perhaps, as lights go up on the space behind the wall. OMAR is at a desk writing. OMAR'S FATHER enters and stands behind OMAR. Perhaps we also hear the sound of someone breathing. OMAR'S FATHER proceeds to do what CINDY narrates:)

CINDY: …with his father—even after he passed away—I remember him telling me once that every time he writes…he feels this—presence. Even after all these years—he feels his father behind him. His hands on his back as he writes. His breath on his neck. And it's not a good feeling. He'll start hyperventilating; because he feels the pressure to…

PATRICK: What?

CINDY: To make it happen. To succeed.

(Lights out on OMAR *and* OMAR'S FATHER. *The wall becomes solid again.)*

PATRICK: Who doesn't. We all do. Get a job and be responsible to your family.

CINDY: I'm not explaining it right. It's a—it's an immigrant thing.

PATRICK: A what?

CINDY: It's like all of it's been this relay race, and it's our turn to carry the baton. We're the ones who have to prove it was all worth it. Leaving home. Living among strangers who don't give a damn about you. It's not all fun and games. It's more a—yeah, it is a responsibility. An obligation. I'm not sure for Omar it's even about being creative anymore.

(Seeing PATRICK'*s reaction.)*

CINDY: I don't expect you to understand.

PATRICK: What's to understand? He needs to prove something to his family. I get that. I spent the first half of my life on a reservation trying to get the hell out and prove myself. I'm not all white.

(From CINDY'*s look:)*

PATRICK: Really.

CINDY: Does your family lay all of their hopes at your door and expect you to carry it for them? We're supposed to be the talented ones. We're the reason they came. Our futures.

PATRICK: How is that different from any other family?

CINDY: Because this is only really our home if we succeed. That's the whole point of uprooting yourself.

PATRICK: Again, I don't see how that's different from anyone else trying to make it.

(CINDY *goes to the fridge and takes out the lasagne.*)

CINDY: It doesn't excuse his shitty behavior for not telling me. He won't be able to write a damn thing if we lose our house. *(She slams the oven door after sliding in the lasagne.)* Jesus Christ. *(Half to herself)* Some days I want to take his fucking notes and throw them in the oven.

PATRICK: Did I miss something? A second ago you were making excuses. Now you want to burn his notes?

CINDY: *(Picks up knife to cut vegetables)* I just—get so mad at him sometimes. I support him. And I know he loves me. But that has to translate into something for once. Why do I have to carry all the weight?

PATRICK: Agreed. I agree.

(CINDY *slams the knife down on a vegetable and starts chopping it for the salad.*)

PATRICK: Easy there. Let's not cut anything off. *(He goes to her to console her.)* You see: the longer you ignore what you want, the more it's going to eat away at you; and that's not going to help anyone.

CINDY: And what would be your solution now that I know we're screwed.

PATRICK: For starters, you can let me help you. You can let me be in your corner.

CINDY: How would that work exactly?

PATRICK: Well, I… *(Making a decision to go for it)* I told you what was on my wish list. As far as—you know— what my goals were. If we're…speaking frankly.

CINDY: What does that have to do with it?

PATRICK: Cindy… *(Levels a look to try and clarify his point)* You asked what my dreams were, I told you. I'm trying to tell you what I…if I could wave a magic wand and make things happen.

CINDY: I don't… *(She plugs into what he might mean, in spite of saying:)* What are you…what are you getting at?

PATRICK: I don't know how obvious I've been in my—feelings towards you. Because I know they're… inappropriate.

CINDY: Rick: I don't need any more drama in my life.

PATRICK: I think that's exactly what you need to get out of this hole you've dug for yourself. You should be dancing in front of an audience. I've been your audience for a while now, and that's just for being the amazing person you are. It's time we got you out of that hole.

CINDY: How? How do I do that?

(Perhaps a high pitched sound begins to filter in. DANCER CINDY is dimly seen behind the wall. She pushes against the wall, which bulges out slightly under her pressure.)

PATRICK: Cindy…I know my opening up like this is wrong on so many levels. And you may think less of me. Because what kind of guy opens up like this to his buddy's wife? But if you were mine… I would do everything to make that dream of yours a reality.

(In manner and movement, PATRICK has been slowly putting the moves on CINDY.)

CINDY: Rick: I flirt. —It's just flirting.

PATRICK: I think it's more than that. You can tell me to back off at any time, and I will. But at least I would've told you how I feel.

CINDY: Rick.

PATRICK: I've always found you, from the beginning—

CINDY: *(Overlapping last few words.)* Telling me how you feel is one thing—

PATRICK: Attractive. *(Perhaps he places his hands around her waist.)* You had to know how I felt about you. And if you don't, it's time I got a little more obvious about it.

CINDY: Don't. Don't get any more obvious.

(PATRICK moves in for a kiss. CINDY moves away to the kitchen table. He corners her there, where he starts to push aside a number of items on the table to make space, placing some of those items on the kitchen table chairs within reach, never moving away from her while doing so.)

PATRICK: I'll give you the space you need. And the time. And the home. So you can do exactly what you want.

CINDY: I think this is just me mad at Omar.

PATRICK: I may be just some guy who works at a moving company, no artist or nothing. But I'm pretty good at figuring out what people want. I have been called "astute" in my time.

CINDY: Astute.

PATRICK: And sharp. And sexy, even. Just so you don't think I'm hurting for company or anything. Also, so you know, I'm great with animals. I have made donations to PETA.

CINDY: Why are you clearing the table?

PATRICK: You can't say no to a guy who likes furry animals.

CINDY: Rick.

PATRICK: You want this, don't you?

CINDY: Not…

(Distracted by PATRICK's lips that hover even closer)

CINDY: …not for the reasons you think I do.

PATRICK: *(He lifts her dress up and pushes her against the kitchen table.)* That's okay if we have different reasons. We have to start somewhere. *(Kisses her neck)* Baby steps.

CINDY: I'm still making dinner.

PATRICK: We'll keep an eye on the lasagne.

CINDY: I don't want to do anything stupid. I—

(PATRICK is still kissing her neck.)

CINDY: —goddamn it…wait…wait.

(Sees a figure through the back door window.)

CINDY: Wait. Fuck, Omar!

(Light change. CINDY sees OMAR standing near the back door entrance. Spot on him. Spot also on OMAR'S FATHER now visible behind the wall. Lights go out on the rest of the stage as CINDY and PATRICK freeze. DANCER CINDY will withdraw her arms and retreat. The father addresses his son.)

OMAR'S FATHER: *(Accent)* Let me tell you something, Omar. You listen good. You listen to your father. From day one I step in this country, they say very clear what they think of us. The people here: they have more love for their dogs than for people like you and me. You see it in their faces, the way they look at you, the way they speak about where we come from. But this—this is our home now. Our home. My sweat is part of this country too. But for all the horse droppings they put in our way, at least this country gives you the shovel. My son, you have talent. I believe in it so much. When I see you work, everything that hurts inside of me, it breaks out into a big smile. Do not follow in my footsteps. You must study more hard than anyone. You must not fail in front of these people. When someone who leaves his country doesn't make it in his new home, if we don't make it, then the ground we stand on, it is not there anymore. You succeeding in their world will give meaning to my eating shit today. Even if this country screws you, it lets you dream big. This is the first and only law of this place. So dream, my son. Dream as big as those motherfuckers who spit on us.

(OMAR *leaves the stage. Spot out on* OMAR'S FATHER. *Lights back to normal as* CINDY *and* PATRICK *unfreeze.*)

CINDY: Omar.

(PATRICK *turns, panicked.* CINDY *moves to the kitchen door and opens it to check.*)

CINDY: Omar? —I thought I just saw him.

PATRICK: You know what, if he sees us, I don't care. Cindy… *(Moves to her)* …I know I should've like— eased into this with even more hints.

CINDY: I'm not going to chuck away my marriage.

PATRICK: It doesn't sound like there's much to chuck away at this point.

CINDY: Did you come tonight with this whole plan in mind?

PATRICK: I never had the guts to say how I really feel until now. It's not easy when it's your buddy's wife you've fallen for.

CINDY: I could never leave him. *(Under her breath)* Even if I sometimes wonder if it isn't something a little—sick that keeps us together.

PATRICK: *(Tries to digest that)* What does that mean?

CINDY: Nothing. Let's leave it there. Everything's already gone too far this evening.

PATRICK: What were you going to say?

(CINDY *shakes her head.*)

PATRICK: Cindy.

CINDY: Never mind.

PATRICK: Just say it.

CINDY: You'll think I'm—no.

PATRICK: Cindy?

CINDY: You'll think I'm terrible.

PATRICK: I won't.

CINDY: It's just… *(Hard for her to say)* I had this—
thought, a few days ago. These thoughts where I…this
crazy idea of…

PATRICK: Would you please just tell me.

CINDY: *(Ashamed to say it:)* Slipping a bunch of sleeping
pills into his beer.

(Slight beat)

PATRICK: When you say a bunch of sleeping pills,
you're not talking about helping him get a really good
night's sleep.

(CINDY shakes her head.)

PATRICK: That's not so bad. Most people when they
get mad enough with someone, they fantasize about
sticking them with a knife, or shooting them. Sleeping
pills sounds really considerate.

CINDY: My life coach said it's normal to have these
kinds of dark thoughts, even about the people you
love. Especially about the people you love.

PATRICK: What happens after you drug him? In this
scenario?

CINDY: He falls asleep. Peacefully. They're great
tranquilizers. I tell myself he'll never have to worry
about failing now. He won't need to carry that burden
anymore. And I won't have to help him carry it. It's

draining to want something so badly and know you
may never achieve it. It eats at you slowly. And then
not so slowly.

PATRICK: Do you get away with it in this scenario?

CINDY: Don't you even dare joke about this with Omar.
This is a private, disgusting thought.

PATRICK: I'm no marriage counsellor, but this feels like
more than a rough patch you're going through.

(CINDY *looks at* PATRICK. *Slight beat*)

CINDY: Rick…I never asked you…. What did you…
what did you get sent to prison for?

(PATRICK *looks at* CINDY. *Slight beat*)

PATRICK: I'll tell you…if you kiss me.

CINDY: I'm serious. I'd like to know.

PATRICK: So am I. Kiss me. And I'll tell you.

(CINDY *looks at* PATRICK. *Beat. She approaches him. She
leans in.* OMAR *appears at the back door and watches as
they kiss.* PATRICK *makes more of the kiss than she intended.
They hear a key rattling in the lock. They quickly break
and move apart as the door opens.* OMAR *enters carrying a
grocery bag.*)

OMAR: Hey. Sorry I'm late.

CINDY: Where were you? I tried calling.

OMAR: I lost track of the time. One minute I thought
I had more than enough time, the next—I'm missing
you, and hurried home.

(OMAR *kisses* CINDY. *He holds the kiss a little too long. She
pushes him away slightly.*)

CINDY: Where were you?

OMAR: Hey Rick.

PATRICK: Hey bud.

OMAR: *(He starts unpacking the grocery bag)* Well—on my way to the store—up on the corner of Jackson and King—did you see the sky about an hour ago? After the rain? The way that low sun was hitting the clouds? Lighting up the wet streets? You couldn't imagine a more beautiful scene if you tried. So—writer that I am, I took that as a challenge. I went to that coffee place nearby thinking I had plenty of time to get home before you got here, and I—tried to write down what I'd seen. That amazing mix of colors; the light bouncing off of windows. And I sat there—I sat there so long trying to come up with something, that I began to be conscious of me sitting there, pen in hand, trying to come up with something. I even started wondering how I must look to anyone watching because I could feel my face pinched in this really concentrated way. This woman, sitting opposite me, I suddenly became self-conscious about how I must look to her, you know, sitting there with my clothes soaked, my hair wet, looking really intense. Even as I tried to capture that sublime scene, I was thinking: "I wonder how I'm coming across to that woman who's watching me." Which completely fucked up the whole sublime thing. *(After unpacking the grocery bag, he starts putting back on the kitchen table the things* PATRICK *had moved when he thought he was going to have sex on it. He puts these items back exactly where they were before being moved.)* Like what a poser, right? And that sudden awareness fucked everything up.

CINDY: *(About the objects he's putting back:)* We were just making a salad.

*(*CINDY *goes to help* OMAR *put stuff back on the table. Near the end of his speech, he will shift the things she puts back to the approximate place they were before* PATRICK *had moved them.)*

OMAR: And each time I was close to finding just the right combination of words, the experience of trying to find those words, the intensity of it, became like the experience. It completely overwhelmed the amazing thing I'd seen. Which made me get even more self-conscious about what I was doing until the sublime thing I wanted to capture completely slipped away from me and I screamed at that woman to please stop looking at me. *(Slight beat)* Then I left. I came back to apologize, really embarrassed, because she had nothing to do with anything of course. I had done this to myself. I had once again not been able to get out of my own way, you know. Which I know I have to do. But I don't know how you're supposed to really do that. How do I get out of my own way and into that—space where you can truly channel the material you want to get to? That stuff that can pour out of your head and make you go "Wow, did I really write that?" Like none of it really belongs to you, but somehow you've been blessed enough to stumble on to it and claim it as yours. And if I can get to that head-space, then I'm gunning it down from the first word to the last. And I just thought, fuck: if this is what I love—how can this love so repeatedly fuck me over? You know. How could it betray me to that extent? I'm committed to this relationship. But what does this sweet love of mine do? Metaphorically speaking? It picks up this knife; *(Picks up a knife)* it picks it up, and then stabs me in the back with it. *(He stabs the table.)* And then picks up this salt shaker and pours salt into the wound. *(He has picked up the salt shaker, and pours it where the knife was plunged.)* And then for good measure, it crushes this chili pepper all around the edges of that wound so that the skin swells up in pain and closes around the wound so I can't even get to the very thing that's hurting me like hell, and that I need to write about. What kind of shitty love is that? I ask you. *(He puts the knife where he remembers it being. Slight beat)* I think this is where it was. This was here, right?

CINDY: What are you doing?

OMAR: I'm putting stuff back where it was. Before he moved it.

(CINDY *and* PATRICK *are looking at* OMAR.)

OMAR: Before he… before he moved it.

CINDY: What are you talking about?

OMAR: Before he cleared the table so he could fuck you on it.

PATRICK: Okay. You know what: first of all: —

CINDY: Can I talk to my husband alone?

PATRICK: First of all, that is a slimy move. That is a creepy-ass slime move. That's voyeur shit. Second of all—

CINDY: *(To* PATRICK*)* Could you go into the bedroom and switch on the T V, or just wait outside, please?

PATRICK: *(Overlapping last couple of words)* That is a misreading of what you saw. That is a flat-out misrepresentation of the facts.

CINDY: Could you leave us alone, Rick? For a second?

OMAR: *(Having picked up a stick of celery and taken a bite:)* I love celery.

PATRICK: What? —What the fuck. How long have you been watching?

OMAR: Watching what?

PATRICK: What the fuck does that mean: "I love celery".

OMAR: I love celery.

PATRICK: I happen to like it too, so what?

OMAR: Good, because it's a particular favorite of my wife's.

CINDY: *(Irritated)* We're not having celery.

PATRICK: I don't mind if you want to, I'm fine with it. I said I want to move out of my comfort zone.

OMAR: Looks like you've gotten off to a good start.

PATRICK: You know what, whatever you thought you saw, you didn't, you just didn't.

OMAR: Denial is not just a river in Egypt.

CINDY: Rick?

PATRICK: You can be such a fucking asshole, you know that.

CINDY: Could you wait outside?

PATRICK: I got nothing to apologize for. Nothing. Everything I said stands, for the record. Just so you know.

(PATRICK *directs his last statement towards* CINDY. *He picks up his beer and a celery stick. He takes a bite as he exits through the kitchen door.* OMAR *and* CINDY *are left alone.)*

CINDY: How long were you watching? —You know something, I don't care. I'm not explaining myself to you. It's you who needs to explain when exactly you were going to tell me you'd been fired? When I couldn't pay our bills? —So your buddy came on to me and for a second I felt turned on by that. Big fucking deal. Shoot me for wanting to live a little for the first time in months. Did you hear the part where I said no because I love you? I don't know why I bother. I don't know what it is about me that makes people think they can take advantage. You're like my family: the more I give, the more they expect from me. That's my job: provider, cook, translator, and all-purpose doormat. And look what you brought from the grocery: it's all for you: Oreos, whisky, soda, chips, beef-jerky, none of this is food. No wonder I almost made out with Rick. Maybe if you spent more time with me I wouldn't be feeling like there's a big gaping hole that needs filling if just to stop me from fucking screaming all the time. *(Unexpectedly she's becomes a little teary)* And you know something…it did feel great to have someone want me again. I feel like a complete lump all day, and you don't help me feel any different. *(Beat. Then:)* Did you hear everything?

OMAR: I saw you guys making out.

(Slight beat)

CINDY: *(Deflecting, by way of explanation)* You know what my life coach said? Ashley?

OMAR: Are you still seeing her?

CINDY: She said I'm suffering from a kind of emotional trauma. She said because I was the one who was always holding my family together growing up, my childhood was a kind of war zone. So that I may very well start expressing that trauma in inappropriate behavior. If some of my needs don't start getting met.

OMAR: Did she say what those needs are?

CINDY: I don't need a fucking life coach to tell me that! You keeping a job is one of them.

OMAR: It's okay you were making out with Rick.

CINDY: How convenient for you you caught me doing that. For the first time ever in the eight years we've been married. Just when I was going to chew you out for getting fired. What a relief for you. Thank God the guilt's on her so I can go on avoiding responsibility for anything. So there was a little groping, big deal. And it was more like an inappropriate hug that went on too long.

OMAR: That hugging was kind of intimate. So was the kissing.

CINDY: That is so creepy you watched that long and did nothing. And I still didn't cross the line in my book.

OMAR: Wherever the line is, I'm saying you don't have to feel bad about it.

CINDY: I don't. I don't plan to.

OMAR: It's a little disappointing, but it's okay.

CINDY: Fuck you and "disappointing". You're the disappointment. And why aren't you more mad? What kind of pussy response is that?

OMAR: I'm trying to be understanding.

CINDY: I would've punched you. If I'd seen you with another woman.

OMAR: It's okay.

CINDY: No it's not. —And how could you lose your job? You think it was beneath you or something? We don't have enough money to think anything's beneath us.

OMAR: Do you know I began to feel envious of the people we were moving furniture for? Each time I moved stuff, it reminded me someone was making a fresh start and I wasn't. I have a home with you, and I don't know why that doesn't mean as much to me anymore.

CINDY: You feel that way? ...This is how you feel?

OMAR: And it has nothing to do with you.

CINDY: You need to talk with Ashley. My insurance covers you. Her advice may sound obvious, but I find when you have to pay for it, the obvious starts to sound really profound and helpful.

OMAR: It's like—if someone could just tell me when do I finally get to feel like there's traction, you know.

That when I put one foot in front of the other there's a good chance I'll end up in a different place from where I started. I don't know if I've fallen down with this thing I'm shooting for, or feeling like I'm not getting anywhere is just part of the struggle.

CINDY: You're in the middle of trying to finish something, that's why it sucks.

OMAR: I've stopped writing. I don't know how to get anything down on paper anymore. I feel so separated from the words I'm using they sometimes feel like a foreign language. I have to keep telling myself it's my language. I have a right to it. I'm not a guest here. Then I tell myself, lighten up. Everyone has their struggle. But I can't figure out what mine is. Not the precise nature of it. I know what my father had to struggle against.

(*Lights up on* OMAR'S FATHER *behind the wall.*)

OMAR: There were borders he had to cross, doors he had to break down. When he punched our walls some nights, I knew why he was punching those walls.

(OMAR *and* OMAR'S FATHER *look at each other.*)

OMAR: I can still see him looking at me when he was in one of his moods. Like I was the weapon. He was going to get his revenge through me. He would show them through me.

CINDY: You have to stop with your dad. He keeps screwing with your head. You don't have to fight his battles anymore. Just the way I refuse to answer to my family the way I used to.

OMAR: (*He takes a few steps towards this memory of his father.*) None of us walk away that easy.

CINDY: But we don't have to be in that head space in the first place.

OMAR: I don't know why his story matters so much to me. Except, you know, it's mine too. Stories matter. Lives vanish like they were never there if you aren't clear about your own place in the world. They just do.

(OMAR *turns back to* CINDY. *Lights out on* OMAR'S FATHER.)

CINDY: But we are clear. I'm clear about the life we're building together.

OMAR: I heard the part where you want to drug me with tranquilizers.

(CINDY *is appalled.*)

OMAR: It's okay.

CINDY: I didn't mean it.

OMAR: If you did it's fine. Again, disappointing, but I understand.

CINDY: Of course I didn't mean it, how could I?

OMAR: I found a bottle of tranquilizers where you keep the cleaning fluids.

CINDY: They're for me. I wanted them in case. Figuring out how to pay our bills doesn't exactly help me switch off at night.

OMAR: Why would you hide them then?

CINDY: I don't want to reach for them automatically.

OMAR: I'm sorry I've put you in a position where you have these violent thoughts about me.

CINDY: But I don't. I'm fighting for us.

OMAR: You must have a few violent thoughts to have a fantasy like that.

CINDY: Well of course I have a few. Don't you sometimes imagine nasty things happening to me?

OMAR: Not really.

CINDY: That's because you're so self-involved you don't even take the time to think of me in a horrible way.

OMAR: I know what you've done for me. Don't think I don't.

CINDY: You won't share anything with me anymore. That's why I'm so mad at you half the time.

OMAR: Don't feel bad about wanting to drug me, seriously.

CINDY: It would be horrible if you thought I meant it.

OMAR: And just so you know: Rick was sent up for manslaughter as a teenager. He punched a guy in a fight. That punch snapped the guy's neck. He went away for five years. —Rick killed a guy.

(Slight beat)

CINDY: Why would you tell me that? *(Then:)* What I said…the whole drug thing—it was like one of those stories you write. It just filled my head for a moment. I don't think I could ever look at you again if you truly thought I felt that in my heart.

OMAR: I'm going to tell you something else. Don't freak out. I took out a life insurance policy for myself. A few weeks ago. If I croak, you're going to be taken care of. I'm going to be a helluva provider when I'm gone.

(CINDY stares at OMAR.)

OMAR: You need to know that in case the insurance guy tries to screw you out of what you're owed.

(CINDY is still staring at OMAR.)

CINDY: Why are you telling me this?

OMAR: I'm saying—all I'm saying—even the darkest thoughts have their, you know—their silver lining. I want to do right by you.

CINDY: I don't understand what you're saying.

OMAR: It's one of those things where you're… where you hope the person understands without necessarily coming to any awkward conclusions—that have to be discussed. If you know what I mean. Otherwise, I know you'd dismiss it before even thinking about it. *(Then:)* I'm saying as far as options go, there's always a way out.

CINDY: But what are you getting at, I still don't understand? *(Getting it, even though she probably got it before)* Honey… Oh, honey. Please tell me I'm just confused.

OMAR: As long as you're getting the drift of what I'm saying.

CINDY: Oh. Oh I see what this is. This is your "fuck you". This is your passive aggressive "fuck you". I'm not going to come storming in like a Neanderthal smashing heads. No, I'm going to fuck with her. I'm going to get in her head and push all the buttons I can think of to make her mad as hell and still come off as the good guy. If only you had the balls to be that insane.

OMAR: I don't seem to have the balls for anything. That's why I took out the policy.

CINDY: Well you know something, after tonight, I might just take you up on that offer.

OMAR: Please. This is what I'm trying to organize.

CINDY: I've wished you dead for like two seconds the entire time I've known you.

OMAR: More than two seconds.

CINDY: But you know what— *(Responding to his last comment)* No, two seconds.

OMAR: Those tranquilizers have been in this house for longer than that.

CINDY: Believe what you want. They're for me, but if you don't have what it takes to deal with your own shit, if you think so little of me and our life together;—

OMAR: I am thinking of you, that's why I took out the policy.

CINDY: Oh my God, I could really kill you right now. I didn't think you were capable of this kind of B S, but this is a new low even for you.

OMAR: Just don't make it seem like a homicide, or you'll get nothing.

CINDY: "Homicide"? Do you want a divorce? Is that what this is about?

OMAR: I want you to stop thinking I'm the worse thing that ever happened to you.

CINDY: When did I ever say that?

OMAR: It pours out of you, all the time, in little ways. I didn't know it was possible to tyrannize another human being with so much selflessness. The way you give of yourself until there's nothing more important happening than what you're doing for the other person. I don't mean that in a snide way but your love seems so dependent on my being a loser that I feel I would be betraying something in our marriage if I actually succeeded. I think you'd be dumbstruck if I succeeded.

CINDY: *(Winded)* I would celebrate.

OMAR: And most of all you can avoid facing your own shortcomings. Am I really the reason you don't pursue your dancing? How handy I must be for that. Maybe you need to keep your dancing just a fantasy because in the cold light of day it doesn't amount to much. You could dance, but could you compete? How good are you really? You never have to find out because your handful of a husband keeps you distracted.

CINDY: How can you be so cruel? To frame everything I do for us in such a disgusting way.

OMAR: I'm trying to free you. You do need to settle down and start your life with a stable, straight-arrow kind of guy like Rick. Now there's a man with a plan. There's something very masculine, and salt-of-the-earth about Rick. And he's management now. He could provide you with the kind of stability you need. And with me out of the way—

CINDY: You're sick. You're turning everything good into something calculating, and evil.

OMAR: I want you to start over. There's no greater magic than starting over, right? Reinventing, going for it. That's what we both talked about when we first met.

CINDY: I have gone out of my way to create a home you can work in.

OMAR: I know: me and your poor family. How they look up to you. The dutiful daughter. That's your real talent looking after sad, struggling cases. Please stop pretending there's some hidden jewel you're hiding that your family or me are stopping you from showing.

(OMAR *sees real pain and hurt in* CINDY's *eyes.*)

OMAR: I know I'm being a shit, I'm sorry. I love you, but sometimes you disappoint me as well. And what I really want now is for you to settle down and be the success story you've always wanted to be; and not just by measuring yourself against me. I'd like to retire my job as the millstone around your neck.

CINDY: You're blocked. You always become an unbelievable asshole when you're blocked. I'm going to pretend you don't mean any of this.

OMAR: I do. Mostly the good parts. The part where you find a better future. Isn't it weird how everyone talks about the future? The present always seems to be too fucked up to say nice things about it. All these songs about a better tomorrow: aren't there any songs about "Oh wonderful present"?

(CINDY *goes to get her phone half way through* OMAR's *speech. He sings a verse from the song* Tomorrow *from* Annie *substituting the word "tomorrow" with "present".)*

CINDY: *(Talks over his singing)* You need to talk with Ashley. The things you're saying now are just ugly.

OMAR: Do you remember when we first met? How young and very green we were. It's strange how two kids who'd been brought up in this country could walk out of that naturalization ceremony and feel like they'd stepped out into something new. That was a brilliant, brilliant day, wasn't it?

CINDY: *(Into the phone)* Ashley, it's Cindy.

OMAR: Hang up.

CINDY: Call me back. I want to make an appointment for my husband. As quickly as you can, please, bye.

OMAR: *(Overlapping)* Cindy. Hang up. It's not going to happen. *(Moves to take the phone from her)* Hang up! Hang it up.

(CINDY *steps away from* OMAR's *reach and hangs up.)*

OMAR: I don't know what happens to my life insurance if I'm deemed *(Makes quotation signs:)* "mentally unstable".

CINDY: You are mentally unstable.

OMAR: But we can't have that be an official diagnosis or they won't pay up. It's a chunk of money. We need the money.

CINDY: There won't be any "we" if the money comes through.

OMAR: There hasn't been much of a "we" for a while now, so what's the difference?

CINDY: Whose fault is that? You don't do anything with me anymore! You barely touch me. You haven't made love to me in months.

OMAR: I can't get a boner, I'm sorry.

CINDY: Why can't you get a boner?

OMAR: I'm a little stressed out. Is the number one reason, I'm guessing. I'll tell you what it feels like sometimes, it feels like I'm at a funeral when I get into bed with you. Like I'm attending my own wake.

CINDY: Why do you feel that?

OMAR: I don't know!

CINDY: God. That is so indulgent; and unattractive. You've become like some artist-wannabe, while the rest of us deal with the boring shit that keeps things running. It's you who's using me as a distraction to keep you from facing your own shortcomings.

OMAR: Okay: this is why I can't get a boner. And this may sound meaner than I intend it to be but: there's something about you as a person recently, sometimes, that's really begun to rub me the wrong way. I stress "sometimes" because most of the time I love you; I do. But like—

(CINDY *will go get a beer, and then go to the kitchen table to chop more stuff for the salad*)

OMAR: —your ambitions for us? All the stuff you want to get? Shopping for furniture we can't afford and then hinting it's my fault that we can't get more in that passive aggressive way of yours. The second car you want, all the goods we apparently swore allegiance to when we raised our hands. The fact that it always comes down to shit we don't have. Stuff we need; the great stack of catalogues, and shopping malls, and credit cards. The lotions you use at night to feel good because the commercial said you would. And now you have the nerve to still talk about wanting to have a career as a dancer? Really? How very inspiring. You can have it all. I'm saying all this because you hate to see me sit on my feelings so this is me sharing. Because at the end of the day I still—I still love you, most of the time. I wish you the best because you're always trying so very hard for us. If only what you were trying so hard for amounted to more than a pile of worthless shit.

CINDY: Thank you for sharing. I know how difficult that must have been for you.

OMAR: I'm sure I'll regret it later.

CINDY: I don't want you to take back a word. You're right: someone needs to cut through our B S. Though I thought the secret to a successful marriage was making the effort to overlook your partner's fuck-ups and huge disappointments, but be that as it may.

OMAR: I was thinking more about everything else you seem to ignore in your pursuit of our happiness.

CINDY: The world starts at home, sweetie; and in the jobs we both need to keep; neither of which you seem to understand. But let me say what is not an issue for me. At least not on the list of the problems we have. The fact that you can't get a boner and function as a man in this marriage for me? Ranks somewhere around your ability to sexually arouse me at the best of times. Which is pretty low. That is not a priority for me. Though yes, while in the past I would never have risked our marriage for it, there was actual physical pleasure when Rick's very hard cock pressed up

against me. I'd forgotten that dicks could get that hard.
And I did, just for a moment, really enjoy that. But
that's an aside.

OMAR: I don't belittle the importance of a working
penis in a successful marriage.

CINDY: What I think may be the real issue here is this
dark, really dark evil crap you're sinking into. The
person I fell in love with seems to have been replaced
by this giant sinkhole that is swallowing everything
good about you, all the light you used to radiate.
You have looked at me these past few weeks like you
wished I'd die.

OMAR: No; that is not true.

CINDY: The contempt in your eyes. Ridiculing what I
want for us. All the things we could finally do once we
were legal. All those seem like fake to you now?

OMAR: I didn't say that.

CINDY: You think I've sold out to something? Have
I failed to carry some memory of hurt the way you
do with your father? I don't need to remember that
kind of pain to function, that's your gig. Forgetting is
healthy. That's the beauty of getting to this country.
We can reinvent everything. Don't blame me if you
can't do it as well as I can. I do remember that brilliant
day. You had the look of someone who had received
the best news ever. I wanted to get next to that person
because I felt it too.

OMAR: We now know what a crock of shit that turned
out to be.

CINDY: I'm doing great thank you very much. In spite
of everything. I'm sorry your family had it particularly
bad. Whose family didn't get treated like second class
citizens because they'd just got here, because they had
just got here.

*(*CINDY *goes to open the fridge. She will look for the salad dressing and take it out. While she does this,* OMAR *will open the cupboard where the cleaning fluids are kept and, unseen by her, take out the tranquilizers.)*

CINDY: We all had to twist ourselves into people we're not to get ahead. That's not a bad thing. It's called adapting. And the price for it is just fine as far as I'm concerned. I like my house. I like the lotions I buy so I can be soft enough to make you want to touch me, you ungrateful shit. And yes, I am a fucking success. I may have to get a second job, and I don't know what the fuck we're going to do about next week's bills, but I am succeeding.

(During the above speech, OMAR *will have gotten a beer, and while* CINDY's *back is turned, he will have quickly poured in the tranquilizer pills.)*

CINDY: In spite of still being considered a second class citizen by some people. I had a patient tell the doctor the other day that he didn't want someone like me touching him. You want to know why I haven't pursued my dancing? Because the thought of it, which is so alive in me, the dream of it keeps me going. Maybe I have been afraid to drag it out into the real world, because it's the only pure thing I can hang onto, and I don't want it soaking up the toxic fumes you live off. God forbid my muse should become as fucked up as yours, screaming at the world all the time. *(At some point, she has swept, or will proceed to sweep, all the salad ingredients into a bowl, and then she will distractedly pour the entire bottle of salad dressing onto the salad, or more than is needed.)* But you know something: I do want to make room for what I love now. And you know something else, of the two of us, I have been the real artist. I've taken a shit sandwich and turned it into something nurturing. I'm the one taking a lousy story and giving it the happy ending I deserve; because

I've fucking earned it. And if you can't be my partner in that then maybe you should just go. Go away and fucking die yourself.

OMAR: We're on the same page then. (*He raises the beer to toast and drinks.*)

CINDY: Oh fuck you and your melodrama. God, how you love to wallow in your own swill. You're like a pig in dirt when it comes to your own pain.

OMAR: I'm trying to come up with a happy ending for you as well. Just give me a second.

CINDY: Oh shut up! What the fuck is wrong with you?

OMAR: I don't know!

CINDY: Then find out! I can't help you if you don't even know what the fuck is going on!

(PATRICK *enters from the kitchen door.*)

PATRICK: I know this conversation is private, but I can't listen to this anymore and not do anything.

CINDY: What's with everyone listening in?

PATRICK: They can hear you two blocks down!

CINDY: We're not done! Get out!

PATRICK: Nah, I'm sorry. I know what's going to happen. You'll finish screaming at him and then you'll try and figure out what's wrong with dear ol' hubby. You'll start feeling all those warm gooey feelings you're programmed to have when a guy opens up to you.

CINDY: Rick?

PATRICK: (*To* OMAR) Some vows like marriage are too sacred. I know that's two-faced coming from someone who just expressed his affection towards your wife. But I was expressing it because I thought it was over, after what happened.

(It takes a second for CINDY *to register the last part.)*

CINDY: After what happened?

OMAR: *(To* PATRICK*)* You don't have to try so hard. You'll win.

CINDY: Win what? What are you both talking about?

PATRICK: I don't want to be the bearer of bad news.

CINDY: That's all you've been this evening.

PATRICK: The messenger always gets killed. Always gets fucking killed. Omar? Would you care to enlighten your wife.

OMAR: I really don't know what you're talking about.

PATRICK: You don't, huh. You don't. *(To* CINDY*)* Remember when you walked in on that talk me and Omar were having about women? The tits and ass discussion, and I got embarrassed and made up some stupid excuse to cover it up? *(To* OMAR*)* Remember now, buddy? You want to continue?

OMAR: I don't feel the need to, no.

PATRICK: *(To* CINDY*)* We weren't talking about just any pair of tits and ass. I was referring to those that belonged to a stripper named Trisha, who also happened to be an accomplished lap dancer.

OMAR: You don't need to do this.

CINDY: What are you both talking about?

PATRICK: *(Continuing)* And the only reason I brought Trisha up is because Omar was telling me about his problems in the bedroom. And I said maybe it's just stress at work, or at home, and if it wasn't anything medical then there was an easy way to find out.

CINDY: What?

PATRICK: I suggested, and it was only a suggestion, that we could go to one of those places for like a, you know, a simple, pre-medical check up to see what was up.

CINDY: You took him to a stripper to see if he could a get a boner?

PATRICK: There was nothing sleazy in my intentions. I was trying to be helpful and save this marriage at the time, believe it or not. I was trying to do a good deed.

CINDY: Hasn't anyone heard of internet porn?

PATRICK: Apparently it wasn't working! So the next step I thought: maybe live girls at a strip club might work.

(Lights up behind the wall. There's now a stripper's pole. TRISHA—played by DANCER CINDY—is going through her dance routine. OMAR—played by OMAR'S FATHER—is seated in a chair with his back to the audience. Club music quietly plays in the background. PATRICK will open the fridge to get a beer at some point. Finding no more beers, he will grab OMAR's beer on the table—or wherever OMAR has put it down next to him—and start drinking.)

PATRICK: So we go to this club. And after a while, I ask Omar if he's feeling aroused in any way, and he says:

MAN-AS-OMAR/PATRICK: I'm not sure.

PATRICK: Aren't you feeling anything? I say to him.

MAN-AS-OMAR/PATRICK: Something; maybe.

PATRICK: —he says. I say to him, Something? Maybe?

MAN-AS-OMAR/PATRICK: She's pretty.

PATRICK: —he says. So then I suggest he should go into the back room and get a private lap dance. I was not encouraging him. I was saying that if his failure in the bedroom is going to torpedo his marriage, then maybe he needs to take drastic measures to find out what the hell is going on. That's all. So—he goes into one of those rooms with Trisha. Now: visual stimulation is one thing, but tactile stuff is a whole other ball game. If I knew such services were being offered I would not have suggested it. Because the next thing I discover as I peek into the room they've retired to: —

(TRISHA *is kneeling in front of* MAN-AS-OMAR, *her head buried in his lap.*)

PATRICK: I'm not going to whitewash this. Her mouth was where you would imagine it would be if you saw a woman kneeling in front of a man. And what is the coup de grass here? (*He mispronounces "coup de grass".*) This man who complained of failure to launch with you, he was not failing to launch. But rather than stopping because he now had his answer, i.e., he could get it up and I was happy for him; now take that boner home and save your marriage. But no, he doesn't stop. Seconds after I stick my head in, he concludes Trisha's oral services by blowing his wad. And boy, did he look happy.

(*The* MAN-AS-OMAR *gasps. Lights out on* TRISHA *and the* MAN-AS-OMAR.)

PATRICK: And that's all I'm going to say. I could say more, but I won't. I don't mean to be the bearer of upsetting news, but you chewed me out for not telling you he was fired.

OMAR: Were you setting me up from the beginning?

PATRICK: Oh. Oh no. You don't push this off on me, buddy.

OMAR: You set me up with Trisha— (*Putting it together*) —and then you see to it I lose my job? All so you could be the bearer of "upsetting news"?

PATRICK: Paranoia is truly the last refuge of assholes. Did I put your dick in Trisha's mouth? No. And I fought for you at work, man. I fought for you.

OMAR: *(Overlapping last few words)* I confide something embarrassing and you see that as an opening to worm your way in? I was trying to set things up for you, you idiot.

CINDY: *(Cold, contained)* What?

OMAR: *(To CINDY)* I know you have a thing for Rick. Watching you two. Jealousy gets to be exhausting after a while. I said, fine, if I'm failing you so bad, let me at least set things right for you financially, and maybe in other ways.

PATRICK: *(To CINDY)* You see, that's why I told you about Trisha, because he pulls this martyr crap and makes himself out to be all self-sacrificing in spite of deep-sixing his vows in another woman's mouth.

OMAR: Was it because of the life insurance I told you about? Is that what triggered this move?

CINDY: *(To PATRICK)* He told you about taking out life insurance?

PATRICK: *(To OMAR)* That was fucked-up telling Cindy what I went to prison for—and then saying you had life insurance. Who's the one scheming here? Hinting that I could be the one to, what? Help her collect? That is so perverted, dude, on so many fucking levels. Making me an accomplice in your wish to self-destruct. Fuck you, man.

OMAR: Everyone would have come out of this with what they wanted if they had just been patient enough.

PATRICK: If I was after your insurance money, why would I bother breaking up your marriage? No, as far as I'm concerned, once a married man comes in a prostitute's mouth, that marriage is over. There's no coming back from that. That's why I started courting Cindy.

CINDY: You really went to a hooker?

(CINDY *underlines the last word by stabbing the cutting board with a knife. The sound heard previously when her migraine came on is heard. A rumbling echo sound could also accompany each stabbing of the cutting board.*)

OMAR: She wasn't a hooker.

PATRICK: Unbeknownst to me, she was a hooker.

OMAR: She was a dancer.

PATRICK: With extra curricular activities that puts her in the hooker camp. Unbeknownst to me.

CINDY: When she went down on you, you still thought she was a dancer? *(She again underlines the last word by stabbing the cutting board.)*

OMAR: *(To* PATRICK*)* Thanks for dragging all this into the gutter.

PATRICK: That was your choice, I'm just relaying the truth.

CINDY: Some sleaze bag whore turns you on but I can't?

OMAR: That's not it.

PATRICK: That's the reason I thought it was over. You need someone who appreciates you.

CINDY: *(As in "shut up":)* Rick?

(Lights up on DANCER CINDY *standing behind the wall, knife in hand. The humming sound starts to increase as the scene goes on.)*

OMAR: I wanted to try anything, do anything to see if I could get unblocked! Then maybe I wouldn't be the emotional and physical mess I am when I'm home with you.

CINDY: Oh, so now the impulse was artistic. You were seeking inspiration.

OMAR: I was trying to get out of my fucking head!

CINDY: I bend over backwards to try and make things work for you, for us—

OMAR: I wish I could take it back, I'm sorry. *(He approaches her, inadvertently placing his hand on the chopping board as he does so.)* I love you. I never want you to think I don't.

CINDY: Don't you dare use that word with me. You've ruined everything. Everything.

(CINDY brings the knife down on to the chopping board where OMAR's hand still rests. He inhales sharply from the shock.)

PATRICK: *(Re: OMAR's stabbed hand)* Oh—shit.

(CINDY looks down and sees what she's done.)

PATRICK: Oh—shit.

CINDY: Oh God.

PATRICK: *(Coming closer to see)* Oh shit.

CINDY: Oh God. Oh God.

(CINDY tugs the knife out of OMAR's hand. In doing so, she ends up butting PATRICK in the forehead with the butt of the knife handle. PATRICK is knocked backwards. He stumbles back against the fridge, or whatever is closet, and slides down. CINDY swivels round to see what she's done, and brings the knife down, and to the side of her, as if to remove it from harming anyone else, but in doing so, and with OMAR positioned behind her, after taking a step forward, the motion ends up stabbing OMAR in the lower stomach. She turns to see this.)

Oh my God. —Oh my God.

(OMAR moves away as he sees the blood on his hand. He tries to steady himself by holding onto a chair, but the chair tilts and he falls.)

(DANCER CINDY *stabs her knife through the "wall", tears open a slit, and enters the living room. The tearing sound is amplified.*)

DANCER CINDY: Thank you. I thought you'd never me let out. I was suffocating in there.

(DANCER CINDY *moves towards* CINDY. *They stand opposite each other.*)

CINDY: Oh my God… oh my God…. All I said was I wanted to dance.

(*Hold for a beat. Blackout*)

END OF ACT ONE

(*Intermission*)

ACT TWO

Scene 1

(From the downstage ceiling area, an oversized American flag unfurls/descends. It is almost like a curtain that covers everything behind it. It could also be a projection of the flag. As this happens we hear many voices giving the United States Oath of Allegiance:)

VOICES: "I hereby declare, on oath, that I absolutely and entirely renounce and abjure all allegiance and fidelity to any foreign prince, potentate, state or sovereignty, of whom or which I have heretofore been a subject or citizen; that I will support and defend the Constitution and laws of the United States of America against all enemies, foreign and domestic; that I will bear true faith and allegiance to the same; that I will bear arms on behalf of the United States when required by the law; that I will perform noncombatant service in the armed forces of the United States when required by the law; that I will perform work of national importance under civilian direction when required by the law; and that I take this obligation freely without any mental reservation or purpose of evasion; so help me God."

(OMAR, now played by the actor playing OMAR'S FATHER, enters. A few moments later, CINDY, now played by the actor playing DANCER CINDY, enters. They both carry their citizenship folder. OMAR inhales.)

CINDY: I felt like doing the same thing.

(OMAR *looks at* CINDY, *wondering what she means.*)

CINDY: Come out here. Take a deep breath. Officially, it's our air now, too. Right?

OMAR: Yes. Yes it is. Congratulations.

CINDY: You too.

OMAR: Omar.

CINDY: Cindy.

(CINDY *and* OMAR *shake hands. They do so in wonder, clearly awestruck by something they've both experienced.*)

CINDY: Well…here we are…citizens.

OMAR: *(Raises his hand)* Citizens. "So help me God".

CINDY: *(Raises her hand)* "So help me God".

OMAR: I wasn't expecting it to be such a—big deal. But—it was a big deal.

CINDY: Yes. Emotional. Really kind of emotional.

OMAR: Yes it was.

CINDY: I thought it was going to be more like some—dry, bureaucratic…

OMAR: Like getting a driver's license.

CINDY: Exactly. Get in line, say something, thank you, I have errands to run, bye.

OMAR: Yeah. Yes, that.

CINDY: Who knew becoming a citizen would be like—a moment. I almost cried. I've lived here most of my life, so—

OMAR: Same here.

(Slight beat)

CINDY: Relief? —We're no longer hanging by a thread? Legally speaking?

OMAR: It feels more than that. Don't you think? I was trying to figure it out myself. It's like…I didn't realize what I didn't have until I was—given it? Like "Oh: this is what I've been missing."

CINDY: Papers. The mother of all papers.

OMAR: No kidding. That too. But— *(Then back to her point:)* Sure: we can walk out now with the rest of the morning crowd. Getting in cars, buses, going to work. Ordinary stuff. Without worrying, but—

CINDY: Claim our share of the American dream.

OMAR: There you go, but. —Why are you smiling?

CINDY: Because I really wanted to share this moment. With someone who'd been through it.

(Slight beat. Then:)

OMAR: *(Still trying to suss out how he feels.)* It still feels so weird though. I kinda feel…I don't know, patriotic? All of a sudden? And I'm not even a "rah-rah" kind of guy. I've always thought of myself as a—citizen of the world.

CINDY: People who say that usually mean they don't feel like they belong anywhere. And not in a good way. Not that I mean you in particular, I don't know you.

OMAR: So what were we this morning before we became citizens? Not quite us?

CINDY: Not quite legal. Being legal is a big deal.

OMAR: *(Thinks about it, then:)* Maybe…maybe that's all it is. Whatever it is, it feels great.

CINDY: Just the fact that I won't be looking over my shoulder anymore. No more us-them. We're them. No: we're us.

OMAR: Did you notice half the room stumbled over the part about bearing arms on behalf of this country. She had to repeat that section.

CINDY: *(A laugh)* Yes.

OMAR: They were thinking, "Are you kidding? We've just escaped from wars. Now you're saying you may want us to go back into one?"—Some of those people came from places this country has gone to war with. Mine. —Yours. *(By way of explanation:)* When they called out your country.

CINDY: We were on the side of the U S though.

OMAR: I tell my dad, if you have issues with this country, why come here, if you can't stand what it did to your home country?

CINDY: What does he say?

OMAR: He says there are opportunities here. But he still has these…resentments. He rants about how we're treated here.

CINDY: Immigrant kids: we're always dealing with our parents' baggage, from back home, literally. It comes with the territory, I guess.

OMAR: But again, so… *(Then:)* I don't know. He says things like holding onto your own history is the only citizenship that matters. Even as he pushes me to become an American. I think for him it's just a place to find work. He doesn't get that I might like—you know, believe in what it might stand for. Even fall in love with it.

CINDY: It's easier for the kids. We don't have as much to remember in the first place. Which is—frankly fantastic.

OMAR: Yes. I think that's what's so exciting to me. It's like we've been given this—brand new…

CINDY: Beginning.

OMAR: Notebook. I was going to say. With all these blank pages. And we can write whatever we want. Our own stories. We don't have to think about anything before today. Now that we're part of this new—well not new, but new for us.

CINDY: I've lived here most of my life, but today I feel that. Which is why these feelings are so—

OMAR/CINDY: —unexpected.

OMAR: Yes.

CINDY: Which is kinda scary and thrilling. Because that means it's all on us now. The family isn't—they're not the only back-up plan anymore.

OMAR: What do you mean?

CINDY: We've been welcomed into another family. Kind of. A much bigger one…. Look at us.

OMAR: What?

CINDY: The way we're talking. So excited. Like we're intellectuals or something. Maybe you are, but—

OMAR: Like converts. Converts talk this way. People born into something don't get it. It's the ones who come to it later in life.

CINDY: Do you know what I was thinking while I was being sworn in? For the longest time I've been wanting to… *(Doesn't continue)*

OMAR: What were you going to say?

CINDY: *(Makes a decision to share)* I've wanted to—dance—professionally. I don't know why today would suddenly make me think, now I can do it. But it's like I've been given permission to do that too. I should add I'm not that good at it.

OMAR: No no: that's not being American. Being shy about your talent is old world stuff. You have to think you're a great dancer. It's written into the citizenship rules that you now have to think big and brash and reach for the brass ring.

(CINDY *laughs.*)

OMAR: That be-all-you-can-be lingo? That's our bible now. None of that third world modesty.

CINDY: "Go for it"; "I am somebody".

OMAR: You know, that's what I'm feeling.

CINDY: You want to be a dancer too?

OMAR: No. But. Why can't you be a dancer? The amount of red tape I went through, and I'm sure you did too, just to get to this point. To breathe. Freely. I don't think anyone who's born here gets that. They think freedom is just normal life. Like running water. They were born with the deeds to their own lives in hand. They don't get what that means; but we do. We actually can taste it; the ingredients. What it takes to become a citizen. Full ownership of our own lives. We can make of it what we will.

(CINDY *is laughing.*)

OMAR: What?

CINDY: So what are you going to do with yours?

OMAR: I don't know. Everything.

CINDY: "Everything". You're going to start there?

OMAR: I'll start with that and work my way up. I'm a writer. I can imagine what I want.

CINDY: A writer. I really admire people who can write. I bet you have a bunch of stories.

OMAR: I do now. —So— (*Gestures:*) Go on, dance. Bust a few moves.

CINDY: Right here?

OMAR: Why not? I'd love to see it.

CINDY: Not in the street.

OMAR: Yes in the street. Celebrate.

CINDY: In public?

OMAR: You want to show the world, don't you? Of course in public.

CINDY: Later. If we ever meet again.

OMAR: Let's meet again now so we can speed up the process.

CINDY: *(Laughs)* That's pretty speedy. Are you sure that's soon enough?

OMAR: No, I don't think that's soon enough. *(Makes a decision)* Cindy: —We don't know each other… and don't think I'm trying to take advantage of the situation, except, I guess I am. I'm going to go for my first brass ring. Something I would never have tried as a non-citizen. I already know I—I like you. And in a couple of minutes I'm going to ask you out for coffee. And much later I will try and—I'm pretty sure, I will try and kiss you. Given that this is the kind of day where I can get away with such a question. Can I, um—can I go ahead and kiss you now? In celebration of what we've been through.

(CINDY laughs.)

OMAR: Instead of after the several dates I'm sure we'll have.

CINDY: Does our citizenship say we can kiss total strangers too?

OMAR: All that fine print is worth reading. All part of jumping into the unknown.

CINDY: Wow, okay. Slick move. I'll give you that. Taking advantage of a moment like this.

OMAR: It's called being enterprising. You too can be just as bold, now that you're naturalized.

(CINDY *and* OMAR *look at each other.*)

CINDY: Have we even shaken hands yet?

OMAR: Done that.

CINDY: So—kissing is definitely the next, logical step in your book.

(OMAR *leans in.* CINDY *and* OMAR *kiss. A light kiss that goes for on for a few moments. They break. Beat)*

CINDY: Everything, huh.

OMAR: The only thing in our way as I see it—is how big we can imagine the rest of our lives.

CINDY: Then stand back… because I plan on putting no breaks on my dreams.

OMAR: Show me. Let everyone passing by see what they can expect from the newest member to their fold.

CINDY: *(Hesitates, then:)* Okay. Screw it. I will.

OMAR: That's the spirit.

(OMAR *takes her citizenship folder. He takes a few steps back to allow* CINDY *to dance. She takes a dance pose, but hesitates again.*)

CINDY: Why not.

OMAR: Don't think about anything else. Just how you see yourself doing what you most want to do for the rest of your life.

(*A low rumbling sound—or perhaps it's the sound associated with* CINDY's *migraines—begins to seep back in.*)

CINDY: *(Psyching herself up)* I'm so ready.

OMAR: It's all about what you want, plain and simple. The wide, open vistas of all you can imagine.

CINDY: I've been ready for the longest time.

OMAR: Ladies and gentlemen, I present to you the great success story you've all heard about, performing the dance of the newly-minted citizen. Drum roll, please… Cindy!

(OMAR *makes an audience-appreciation noise as the rumbling/ migraine sound increases. The lights fade out on young* OMAR *and* CINDY. *Lights go up behind the flag showing the older* OMAR *and* CINDY. OMAR *is either on the floor, or perhaps at the kitchen table, getting his stomach cut stitched up by* CINDY. *A medical first aide kit is nearby.* PATRICK *is nearby with an ice-pack on his forehead.*)

(*The flag rises. It can also fall into the hands of the younger* CINDY *and* OMAR *and be carried out by them. If it's a projection, it fades out. As the flag disappears, the younger* CINDY *and* OMAR *turn and see their older selves. They cross the stage and exit looking at their older selves.*)

Scene 2

(CINDY, OMAR, *and* PATRICK *are in the kitchen as described above.* OMAR *has his shirt open as* CINDY *stitches the wound on the side of his stomach.* OMAR'*s hand has already been bandaged.*)

PATRICK: He's fine. It didn't go in that deep. You nicked him. I'm the one whose head got bashed.

CINDY: I didn't hit you that hard. Your forehead's fine.

PATRICK: You head-butted me with a steel knife. I may have got brain damage or something.

CINDY: *(To* OMAR*)* Am I hurting you?

OMAR: No.

PATRICK: Look. I'm sorry I took him to a strip joint. But he's a grown man. He could have abstained from what happened in that room. I swear I went there just to see if your husband could be a functioning guy for you. *(To* OMAR*)* Didn't I say let's go see if everything's operational for Cindy's sake?

OMAR: *(To* CINDY*)* He was very concerned about your sexual satisfaction.

PATRICK: Don't say it like that, like I'm some perv.

OMAR: He was concerned about my getting hard for your sake.

PATRICK: It was a testament to my moral character that I put aside my feelings for Cindy for the sake of both of your happiness, motherfucker. I just didn't realize at the time you'd lost your mind. Plotting some bullshit behind the scenes like some mental retard. Except you know what, I don't believe it for a second, that whole life insurance, use-Rick-to-off-me suicidal b.s. Give me a break. No wonder you're a failure as a writer if that's the kind of plotting you come up with. But okay, let's take him at his word. We're all on the same page then: he wants to hit the nuke button on himself. He's practically pushing you into my arms. I want you. You're attracted to me, don't tell me you're not, what is the problem? *(To* OMAR*)* So I anticipated your wishes before you formally declared this marriage was over. But it's over. I don't mean to be judgmental, but you don't need to be a genius to see the spark has fizzled between you two. The flame of love has been pissed on and is out. Am I wrong? I know I should've said how I feel before you had to witness what happened. Which I didn't anticipate happening tonight, by the way. But at the end of the day, you want what's best for Cindy. Am I right?

OMAR: I do.

PATRICK: That's why I ultimately respect you, man. Because you're someone who seeks the truth even if it doesn't shine a good light on you. *(To* CINDY*)* You need to hear what he's saying. We can all be civilized about this. We can get him the mental health specialists he needs. *(To* OMAR*)* No disrespect to you but you're having trouble, buddy. And that's no reason to drag someone you once loved down with you.

OMAR: Thank you for being there.

PATRICK: Okay, but you don't have to be sarcastic about it. I'm trying to be sincere here.

OMAR: So am I.

PATRICK: People's happiness is at stake.

OMAR: I still love her.

PATRICK: *(Thrown off for a second)* But—that's like—poison at this point. You may think you're still serving wine in this relationship but you're handing her a glass of vinegar every day.

CINDY: *(Finishes putting a bandage on* OMAR*'s wound)* Could you leave us alone again, Rick? Please?

PATRICK: No. Uh-uh. You don't know what it's taken for me to finally share with you how much you mean to me. We told each other what we wanted, and I'm not about to flush that away because hubby here is pulling this wounded shit at the last minute.

OMAR: I am wounded.

PATRICK: I'm bleeding too.

CINDY: You're not bleeding.

PATRICK: *(Showing her the cloth-covered ice-pack)* What's that?

CINDY: That's red dye from the cloth.

PATRICK: It's blood.

CINDY: The cloth has red patches.

PATRICK: You're saying that to make it seem less bad than it is.

CINDY: Go into the bathroom and look.

(PATRICK *draws* CINDY *close to him. She may try to push him away, but he stays physically close to her.*)

PATRICK: Cindy. I love you. I know being candid is awkward with your husband present, but I think Omar is open to hearing it like it is.

OMAR: I am. Candor is always refreshing.

PATRICK: You two got married when you were young. Things crash and burn. That's no reflection on Omar. But a wise man once said: "move on". That's wise counsel few people listen to.

CINDY: Rick—

PATRICK: No. You don't know what "seize the day" means anymore. You always have an excuse to put off what you want.

CINDY: This is my fault. I spoke of something I shouldn't have. I'm actually a pretty lousy dancer.

PATRICK: No. Don't say that.

CINDY: That's why I never continued.

PATRICK: Being around a sinking ship will do that to you. It will drag down everything in its wake. No offense, man, but we're talking about someone we both care about.

OMAR: Go for it.

CINDY: Shut up.

OMAR: We should hear him out.

PATRICK: No one's talking behind anyone's back here. I think you both want out but don't know how. It's

normal: couples hit a wall and ask, does the person I'm
with help me feel good anymore? Or am I miserable
as fuck and ready to shoot myself? This is for Omar's
well-being as well.

OMAR: This is like going to your life coach without
leaving the house.

PATRICK: Yeah, and she would agree with me. It's like
my mother who was stuck in a marriage that should
have ended.

(CINDY *rolls her eyes and reaches for the can of beer with
the tranquilizers that* PATRICK *had been drinking.* OMAR
reaches out to stop her from drinking it.)

OMAR: Cindy

PATRICK: No—

(CINDY *shakes it, realizes it's empty, and takes it to the trash
can.*)

PATRICK: —listen. You both can't see it because you're
in the middle of it. Why people hang onto something
that's like broken, I don't know. No, I do—

(CINDY *looks in the oven at the lasagne.*)

CINDY: Well this evening's totally fucked.

OMAR: The night's young.

PATRICK: Let me finish.—

CINDY: I'm sorry for stabbing you; I don't think I
officially apologized.

OMAR: You were upset, understandably.

(CINDY *opens a cabinet and takes out a whiskey bottle and
three glasses. She will pour drinks in all three glasses. She
will give, or slide a glass on the table to the two men.*)

PATRICK: (*Continuing*) You hang on even when it's over
because otherwise you think it was all for nothing.
Could I have been that stupid to hang onto something

that beats the shit out of me emotionally? But it only becomes a reflection of your intelligence when you don't move on.

CINDY: Again, this is my fault. I led you on. I shouldn't have said anything.

PATRICK: Omar: do you give Cindy permission to truthfully say what's in her heart?

CINDY: I don't need his permission.

OMAR: I'd like to hear it.

CINDY: *(To* OMAR*)* You would, would you?

PATRICK: You're artists. Aren't you people all about telling it like it is.

OMAR: Not necessarily; depends on the day.

PATRICK: *(To* CINDY*)* Tell me you don't feel something for me. I know you'll say it's only, you know, sexual. Like that means nothing. But okay, let's go there. There is a real sexual thing between us. Isn't there? Even Omar witnessed that.

OMAR: I did. I wanted to machine-wash my eyes afterwards.

PATRICK: Please don't discourage her speaking her mind.

OMAR: Pretend I'm not here.

PATRICK: *(To* OMAR*)* Thank you for being open to this, you're the bigger man for it. *(To* CINDY*)* I heard you talk about, you know, enjoying—that. I'm not a flash-in-the-pan when it comes to knowing how to give pleasure to someone I love. That's high up on my list of things owed to a partner.

(CINDY *looks like she's ready to dismiss the experience.)*

PATRICK: Please, speak from your heart. You like me. Don't you?

CINDY: Yes, I like you.

PATRICK: No. I mean you like me. In the way you know I mean.

(CINDY *looks like she might be ready to dismiss* PATRICK's *point altogether, but then stops and looks at him. Looks at him like she might be really tuning in to what he's saying.)*

PATRICK: I'm not so stupid to think you might love me. We haven't taken a big enough step down that road for you to feel anything like that now. But: you like me, right?

(CINDY *continues to look at* PATRICK.)

CINDY: Yes… Yes, I suppose.

PATRICK: Do you know how many times in a day I hold you in my thoughts. Imagining the life we both could have. The life I could make for you. That you could make for yourself with my help.

(Small beat)

OMAR: Okay, now I'm getting uncomfortable. Am I supposed to leave the room?

CINDY: *(To* OMAR*)* This is as much your doing.

PATRICK: *(Determined to make his case)* Nobody wants to hurt Omar. Beyond his mental issues, he's a good guy.

OMAR: Thank you.

PATRICK: I just want you to stop hurting. This dream of dancing, it's just one of the many things that's like waiting to explode out of you. That needs to explode out of you. And I know you'll say whatever feelings you have for me won't last because I'm just a side thing. The shiny new thing that's always good in the beginning. I know I'm presuming a lot, but—Cindy: *(He takes her hand, or just comes close to her.)* I can make a life for you. I can help you take the next steps you're dying to take. I am the brand new, shiny thing.

That's not a bad thing. That's starting over. To know everything's possible again. Goals, hopes, everything. Bills can be paid. What you're going through doesn't have to be rest of your life.

(OMAR *has been watching this with increasing tension as he sees* CINDY *listening to what* PATRICK *is saying.*)

PATRICK: I'm not asking you to make a decision now.

OMAR: No; I think you should make a decision now.

PATRICK: *(Ignoring* OMAR*)* Why can't you have what you want? Do you understand what I'm saying to you.

OMAR: Listen to the man. Rick here is the shiny new thing. And I have every expectation he'll keep being shiny even after the honeymoon phase is over. I mean look at him. Weren't you All American in high school?

PATRICK: You know what: —

OMAR: *(Interrupting)* Though I think you should amend the whole reservation angle. One hundredth part Cherokee, and a hippy aunt who took you to live with the Native Americans doesn't make you Native American.

PATRICK: I'm part Chehalis, for your information, and it was my father who took me there.

OMAR: Your hippy father. You're about as Native as every other white guy who pretends to be Indian. I don't bring up that tall tale as a negative, I'm complimenting you. You're like a catch, if you have low financial expectations. A manager at a moving company doesn't exactly make you Bill Gates.

PATRICK: It's a regular paycheck that covers a mortgage, unlike you.

OMAR: What I'm saying is in spite of some speed bumps in your resumé, you are a catch. Even an

example for sad cases like me who still have those
sneaky questions about whether they fit in or not.

CINDY: Let's sit down for dinner, shall we. *(She will
proceed to loudly, aggressively—with plates, cutlery—set
the table for dinner.)*

OMAR: Even though the beauty of becoming an
American, supposedly, is never having to say you're
sorry for being whoever you were before becoming an
American.

CINDY: I'm glad to see you've recovered enough to be
obnoxious.

OMAR: Stabbing me just made me light-headed,
sweetie. But putting aside my obnoxiousness, you
should seriously think about Rick's offer.

PATRICK: Didn't you say you wanted Cindy to have a
better life?

OMAR: I'm trying to sell you to her, buddy.

PATRICK: I don't see how sarcasm helps that.

OMAR: That's because we're all a little too fucked up
at the moment to catch the sincerity in our voices. I'm
saying let's look at the qualities you possess and that
I never could. And I'm only speculating that may be
because you are truly of this land. None of these fresh-
off-the-boat, Omar-come-lately types that take the
shine off of the true inheritors of these "beautiful for
spacious skies".

CINDY: Is that what you think all this is?

OMAR: I have an inkling of your fantasy life. How you
look at some guys. I don't mean to bring race into a
polite conversation.

CINDY: That's your excuse now for your failure? It's
all because you're a foreigner? Seriously? Even your

father who told you to fight would be embarrassed by
that.

OMAR: So you're admitting I'm a failure?

CINDY: You're the one who's made that decision.

OMAR: And I'm saying in case I don't quite measure
up anymore, let's look at the great salesman here that
could be my replacement.

PATRICK: *(To* CINDY*)* You don't have to listen to this; we
can leave.

OMAR: I'm here to celebrate you, Rick. I want to speak
of your great qualities. Yes, in comparison to me, how
else do we measure people but against each other.
No one's good, or amazing, or anything unless they
are measured against others who bomb in the same
thing. There have to be failures in order to notice the
successes.

PATRICK: Cindy. We can go.

*(*CINDY *continues setting the table.)*

OMAR: *(Continuing)* Nothing more human. Even
you with your truly insignificant life, you're still a
greater success than me. You're having a much greater
success at just living. Of truly chewing the fat out of
everything. You like channel all the wonderful bullet
points of every motivational speech that was ever
written with just enough sin and adultery to make you
interesting.

PATRICK: Alright, just, whatever, man

OMAR: *(To* CINDY*)* This is a catch.

CINDY: *(To* OMAR*)* You're so pathetic.

OMAR: This is a man with a plan, and an erection. None
of those deadly doubts that plague those of us who
wonder if we have a right to anything. Because at the

end of the day, I mean, who the fuck do I think I am? Right?

CINDY: Yes. Let's go. I'll pack a bag.

PATRICK: Do you want me to help you?

CINDY: I'll be right back.

(CINDY *has turned away and doesn't see* PATRICK *stumble, and try to steady himself by the kitchen table. She exits into the bedroom.*)

OMAR: *(To* CINDY *as she exits. Then to* PATRICK *after she leaves.)* But Rick here: sturdy, rugged; almost like a Mount Rushmore impersonator, if there was such a thing. Virile, free of burdens, who carries nothing more on his back than common sense, the common consensus, the common good, common everything really.

PATRICK: I don't feel so well.

OMAR: You are one of the blessed. You truly get to live the myth and promise of everything this country has to offer. I'm not saying I can't. But the fact is you just manage to do it so much better.

PATRICK: *(Feeling groggy)* All's fair in love and war, man.

OMAR: Yes; yes it is. And I'm not going to stand in the way of the great Darwinian imperative that says people like you need to get the girl for the sake of the greater good.

PATRICK: You can't take care of her like I can.

OMAR: I have no doubt you will dote on her.

PATRICK: Can I give you some friendly advise?

OMAR: I sense that's not a question.

PATRICK: You need to work on your interpersonal skills, man. You suck at it, big time.

OMAR: I will take the next few lonely and wifeless years to reevaluate my social skills.

PATRICK: I don't mind hanging out with you, but others find you a little intense, to put it politely.

OMAR: Well let's be honest, you hung out with me to get close to Cindy.

PATRICK: No; I like you, man, when you're not being a bitch.

OMAR: But I was still your way to get into my wife's pants.

PATRICK: I love her; and I'll take care of her.

OMAR: I'm not saying your heart's not involved, but her tits and ass figure into this.

PATRICK: Well of course they do, she's a beautiful woman. But you just dropped the ball with her. You don't know how to take care of her anymore.

OMAR: You don't really give a shit about her dancing, do you.

PATRICK: You come back in a year and see where she is after living with me.

OMAR: I really wish I could be you. There's something almost Disney-like about you. The way your being so deeply empty-headed seems so strangely attractive to people.

(OMAR *will get a little too close to* PATRICK, *forcing* PATRICK *to move away.*)

OMAR: People genuinely like you. And I find that kind of offensive. I don't know why the lowest common denominator always seems to win out. Not when people say they're shooting for something better. If I could just crack that, if I could just understand why lug heads like you are the real winners in life, I think I could finally start making it.

PATRICK: *(Feeling wobbly on his feet)* I'll tell you something for free: the key to success is not being an asshole.

OMAR: You think so? Because I feel like I've just started exploring my full potential as an asshole. I feel I could finally shine in that capacity.

PATRICK: What the fuck. I feel dizzy.

OMAR: It must have been that celery. Too much celery acts like a narcotic.

PATRICK: *(At the sink)* I think I'm going to pass out.

OMAR: Before you do, I have to ask you: did you really think I was just going to let you walk out with my wife?

PATRICK: What the hell. You said you wanted what's best for her. You said it was okay.

OMAR: Yes: I have aspirations for being selfless. But in practice, seeing your hands paw at my wife really burnt a hole in my eyes. I actually felt the edges of my retina crinkling like burnt paper. Watching all that pleasure light up in her. I really did think I could will myself out of the picture. I mean that seems like a good story. A beautiful ending to me. Sort of like a *A Star is Born* where the guy sacrifices himself so the real talent in the relationship can get ahead.

PATRICK: Shit. I'm going to pass out.

OMAR: But seeing your hands all over her? It just snuffed out those selfless aspirations and made me want to cut off your dick. In fact: *(He picks up a kitchen knife.)* Why wait until you've passed out? We should all be awake to the really important moments in our lives.

PATRICK: Get the fuck away.

OMAR: I'll be quick. It'll be clean. Chopping salads for my wife all these years has made me an expert. Look:

(He takes a stick of celery and chops it, flicking the chopped bit onto the floor.) It'll be that clean.

(More wobbly now, PATRICK *collapses onto the floor. As* OMAR *moves towards him,* PATRICK *tries to crawl away.)*

PATRICK: Cindy. Cindy! Help.

OMAR: Don't be scared. Just take out that joy-stick of yours and I'll show you. Show me that magic wand.

*(*OMAR *slashes the air over* PATRICK'*s crotch at certain points.* PATRICK *tries to protect his crotch with his hands.)*

OMAR: That pleasure provider. That adultery enabler. Your buddy betrayer. Your knife-in-the-back maker.

PATRICK: Cindy.

OMAR: *(Overlapping)* Your monkey spanker. Your joy-to-my-wife. Your fuck-you-I've-never-been-limp-in-my-life stick. Your All-American manhood, bitch.

PATRICK: Cindy! Help!

OMAR: How successful do you think you'd be without your prick? I have to be honest: I'm feeling real animosity towards your privates right now. You, personally, I don't mind. But I'm really miffed at the thought of all your future erections, especially as they relate to my wife.

PATRICK: Cindy!

OMAR: *(Mocking voice)* "Oh Cindy, help me". Who needs rescuing now?

*(*CINDY *enters with a suitcase.)*

PATRICK: Cindy. He's trying to cut my dick off. He's gone fucking psycho.

OMAR: I don't know about psycho. I was thinking about snipping some of it off.

CINDY: Omar?

OMAR: Yes, sweetie?

CINDY: Can you drop the knife?

OMAR: You're one to talk. Stabber of hubby.

CINDY: Omar?

OMAR: Oh sure. No biggie. I was momentarily overcome by that green-eyed monster. *(He puts the knife down.)* You never know when it will sneak up on you. But you two love birds should definitely skedaddle. Do you want some of this dinner to go?

(CINDY has already gone over to PATRICK.)

CINDY: Why are you on the floor? What happened?

PATRICK: That knife-butt to the head. I told you.

OMAR: Mixing beer and whiskey. Never a good idea.

CINDY: Can you stand up?

PATRICK: Everything feels like it's underwater.

CINDY: *(To OMAR)* What did you do to him?

OMAR: Okay, fine, I'll fess up. He drank a beer full of those tranquilizers. The same tranquilizers you fantasized about using on me.

(CINDY stares at OMAR to see if he's kidding.)

OMAR: I was going to drink it myself in a grand, dramatic gesture. A big farewell.

(CINDY rushes to the cabinet where she had placed the sleeping pills.)

OMAR: But then he started in talking about the lap dancer and I thought, you know, shut the fuck up.

PATRICK: Wha—?

OMAR: I thought if you're going tell her I got a b.j. to turn the person I love against me— *(He goes to the trash can and retrieves the empty bottle that held the pills. He shows it to her.)*

PATRICK: I'm going to die.

OMAR: —then fuck you too.

PATRICK: I'm going to die.

OMAR: Well they can't be that effective, you're still alive.

PATRICK: This is fucking it, man. Oh shit, oh shit, I'm going to die. I'm too young.

(CINDY *has rushed to help* PATRICK *to his feet.*)

OMAR: You're not going anywhere. I planned on saying what you'd drunk, eventually. I wasn't going to let you die.

CINDY: You need to throw up. You need to throw it all up.

OMAR: I still wish the best for both of you. In the part of me that isn't jealous. In fact let me help. (*He goes to take* PATRICK's *other arm.*)

PATRICK: (*Pushing* OMAR *away*) Keep him the fuck away from me.

CINDY: Let him help.

(CINDY *and* OMAR *both help* PATRICK *to the bathroom.*)

PATRICK: He's fucking psycho. He's going to do a murder-suicide on us. Call the police.

OMAR: It was just you I wanted to murder. But I'm over it.

PATRICK: Call the police.

(*We see them enter the bathroom. The toilet is either visible, or we will just see* PATRICK's *bottom half as he hugs the off-stage toilet to throw up.*)

CINDY: Here, get him—help him down. Get his head over the bowl. Stick a finger down your throat. Rick?

You have to stick your whole hand down your throat and throw up what you can. I'll be right back.

(CINDY *rushes back into the kitchen. She fills a glass with water. She uncaps the salt and dumps it all in. She pours in some whiskey. Then she picks up the mustard on the table and squeezes as much as she can into the glass. She stirs it all up with a utensil and walks back to the bathroom. While she's doing that:)*

PATRICK: Don't leave me with him.

OMAR: I can help you stick a hand down your throat.

PATRICK: Get off.

OMAR: Stick all your fingers in. Seriously, you need to do it. That's it. Shove it all in. Choke on it.

(PATRICK *retches loudly.)*

OMAR: There we go. Out it comes. Doesn't that feel better? *(To* CINDY*)* He's doing it. He'll be alright. *(To* PATRICK*)* Shove your hand back in. Here, let me shove mine.

PATRICK: Get off me.

CINDY: Leave him alone.

OMAR: I'm helping him vomit.

CINDY: *(Moving back into the bathroom)* Move aside. Patrick? I need you to drink this. Take the glass. Drink it all up.

PATRICK: What is it?

OMAR: It's yummy.

CINDY: It'll help you vomit. Chug it. You have to chug it.

(PATRICK *gulps it all down. His face contorts into one of absolute disgust. He directs a wounded gaze at* CINDY, *before turning back to the toilet bowl and retching even more loudly.)*

OMAR: He did say he was trying to move out of his comfort zone.

(CINDY *looks at* OMAR.)

OMAR: I was going to say something before it did any harm. It didn't do much for me, the couple of sips I took. It just kind of numbed the pain for the stabbing. Lucky, huh.

CINDY: Just keep throwing it up.

OMAR: He'll be okay. He's fine. (*About something else:*) Cindy: —look.

CINDY: (*To* PATRICK) Stick your fingers down your throat again if you need to.

OMAR: Cindy?

CINDY: Get it all out.

OMAR: Cindy?

CINDY: What?

OMAR: (*Pulling her away from the bathroom*) Please— uhm. Please don't…don't go. Don't leave with him. Don't—don't leave. Period. If you want to go, of course, go. But—please don't. I didn't mean to hurt him. A little—maybe. But no more than—you know. Accidentally. All of tonight's been a huge misfire from the moment I walked in. Everything I've said that isn't about how much I love you is the opposite of what I'm feeling. It's scary how I can feel something so deeply and yet hear myself say the opposite of that. I love you. That's behind every stupid thing I've said tonight. And I've failed at that. And I don't know how to fix that. Plus, I'm blocked. I've been having a really shitty few months staring at blank sheets and wondering how I'm supposed to pull the rabbit out of that hat, when there doesn't seem to be a rabbit anymore, and not even a hat. I see you work so hard and make something of yourself and I'm proud of you. You've done it and I—I promised so much to you and I've come up short.

CINDY: I wasn't looking for a super hero.

OMAR: I wasn't shooting to be one. I was just hoping to measure up to something. You know. Carry my share.

(A particularly loud retch from PATRICK. CINDY *looks over at* PATRICK. *We also begin to see smoke emerge from the oven.)*

OMAR: You'll be okay, Rick. Purging is good for you now and again.

PATRICK: *(Weakly)* Fuck you.

CINDY: What's that smell?

PATRICK: Don't listen to that pile of horse shit coming from—

*(*PATRICK *dry heaves, as* CINDY *runs to the kitchen oven.)*

CINDY: Oh shoot. Shoot.

*(*OMAR *follows her into the kitchen as* CINDY *opens the oven. Black smoke billows out of the oven. The smoke alarm goes off.* OMAR *puts on oven mittens.)*

OMAR: I've got it. I've got it, move.

*(*OMAR *takes out the burnt lasagne and places it on the kitchen table as* CINDY *opens the back door, and a window. He waves a dish cloth in front of the smoke alarm. They turn to look at the lasagne for a couple of beats. He takes a fork and pokes underneath the burnt top. The smoke alarm stops.)*

OMAR: It's only the top. It's fine underneath.

(The evening's emotional turmoil is evidenced momentarily in CINDY's *demeanor.)*

CINDY: The crispy top is the best part.

OMAR: Well…it's crispy.

(Another dry heave from PATRICK. *Slight beat)*

OMAR: Honestly—to be honest. I think I would…it would be very difficult without you…. I don't want that to put pressure on you or anything.

CINDY: It won't.

OMAR: Because I'm not—I'm not going to beg. Begging is just so unattractive. Unless begging might work? In which case, I'm begging. I don't know if what we have is even love anymore. I know that's gotten pretty beat up. Nothing gets beat up more than love. But I do know my life only truly started with you. And I can't imagine it without you. I'd survive. But in that barely functioning way of people who survive a catastrophe, you know.

(There's a gesture or a look from CINDY *that suggests that what* OMAR *is saying is all too late. Either she shakes her head slightly, or looks away and slightly shakes her head, or leans her elbows on the table and puts her face in her hands.)*

OMAR: I'm pretty sure I'll think of a bunch of stuff after you've left. I know there's one good argument, one really persuasive thing to say that I haven't thought of yet. So while I'm waiting for that really persuasive thing, can you just pretend I've said it? And be moved? And impressed? And just stay.

*(*PATRICK *stumbles out of the bathroom.)*

OMAR: Please?

PATRICK: And I thought I was the only one vomiting. At least my excuse was that I was poisoned. *(To* CINDY*)* And you stand there and listen to all that shit? Am I the only one standing up for you in this house? Because you don't seem to be doing it. *(To* OMAR*)* And just so you know, I'm suing you. For attempted homicide. I am going to shove the legal system so far up your ass you will be shitting lawyers. I am going to see you so fucking deported and your citizenship revoked. Oh man. You have no idea what I'm going to do. You think you're getting away with this just because I didn't die? Nah, man; I regard it as my civic duty to see your ass thrown in jail. You are a plague, buddy. This country used to be something before they opened the floodgates to people like you, who just take and take and then cry about how they're treated.

OMAR: *(To* CINDY*)* See, he's much better.

PATRICK: Keeping down good people like Cindy. So that she ends up feeling like she isn't the amazing person she is. *(Picks up* CINDY's *suitcase)* Thank God I came to dinner tonight. Thank God. This has turned out to be like a fucking rescue mission. I feel like a goddamn SEAL team parachuting in to extract a hostage. *(To* CINDY*)* You're welcome.

*(*PATRICK *looks at them for a second like he might continue. Then he passes out.* OMAR *and* CINDY *don't move for a few seconds, wondering if this isn't part of* PATRICK's *way of concluding his speech.)*

CINDY: Oh crap. He's passed out. *(Moves to* PATRICK*)* Call 9-1-1.

*(*CINDY *stops when* PATRICK *stirs and sits up, groggy.)*

PATRICK: And for the record. He came twice in that hooker's mouth. Once may be going with the flow, but twice? Twice makes it a premeditated orgasm. That's ejaculation with intent. I'm sorry to be the one to break the news and I know I'm not at my best right now; and in case I pass out again… *(Senses he's about to pass out again)* please don't let my vomiting be the last thing you remember about me. *(He looks at her pleadingly.)* I love you…you will never stop dancing with me. *(He continues to look at her for another moment and then passes out.)*

CINDY: I'll drive him to the hospital.

OMAR: I'll come with you.

CINDY: No. Just help me get him to the car.

(Together, CINDY and OMAR lift PATRICK's body.)

OMAR: I'll tell them what happened.

CINDY: I'll handle it.

OMAR: I don't care what happens to me.

CINDY: It won't get to that. Just help me carry him.

(CINDY and OMAR lift/drag PATRICK to the kitchen door.)

OMAR: He'll be okay. He's survived drinking binges like you won't believe.

(They exit. If more dialogue is needed to cover the time it takes to exit: Cindy: You've got him? Omar: I've got him, keep going. Cindy: Don't drop him.)

(We hear cars doors being opened.)

CINDY: *(Off-stage)* I'll take it from here.

OMAR: *(Off-stage)* I'll go with you.

CINDY: *(Off-stage)* No, I've got it.

OMAR: *(Off-stage)* You sure?

CINDY: *(Off-stage)* Yes.

(OMAR appears at the kitchen door still looking off-stage at the departing CINDY.)

OMAR: Are you coming back? …Are you coming back? …Cindy?

(A car door slams. The engine starts. The sound of a car driving off. OMAR stares off-stage for a few moments, then walks back into the living room. He sits down. Beat. Lights down)

Scene 3

(Transitional music or sounds. In the dim light we see
OMAR *pick up a nearby notebook and start writing.)*

(The lights fade up as the sound of a car pulling in is heard.
It is morning now. Sunlight. OMAR *gets up, turns to the*
kitchen door. CINDY *enters. She places the car keys on the*
kitchen table.)

OMAR: How is he?

CINDY: *(Gets a glass of water)* We pumped his stomach.
—He's awake. —They're keeping him for a day. He'll
be okay.

OMAR: I knew he would be. *(Slight beat)* I'll apologize
to him. Some time.

CINDY: You do that.

(A moment, then:)

OMAR: Did they ask what happened?

CINDY: I know the doctor. I spoke to him. I told Rick if
he wanted any chance with me he'd have to stick to the
story I gave them.

OMAR: I don't want that to be the reason you go with
him.

CINDY: I'm not going with him. *(Slight beat)* I'll speak to
him later. When he's feeling better.

(A moment, then:)

OMAR: After I smooth things over with him…we
should have him over for dinner again. *(Then:)* Or not.
—Maybe it would be too awkward. *(Slight beat)* I saw
a help-wanted sign at the coffee shop. —I'll check it
out today. —There's another moving company that's
hiring, in case. I'm feeling pretty motivated. —I guess
I—I needed to get it out of my system. Vomit out
whatever it was I needed to vomit. *(A moment, then:)* I'll

get it together. —I even started making a few notes for
a new novel while you were gone. I haven't given up.
—That's what I'm trying to say.

(Slight beat)

CINDY: Did I ever tell you why I wanted to be a dancer
in the first place? I don't think I did.

(OMAR shakes his head.)

CINDY: I realized that driving home…. It wasn't like it
was something just dying to get out. —It was these—
young girls from the ballet school next to my father's
store. They would come in for soft drinks. And candy.
They were all so… pretty. Their cute outfits… *(During
the above speech, she will go over to the burnt lasagne still
on the table. She will pick up a fork and remove the burnt
parts so as to get to the edible areas. She will take small
bites.)* Their hair in those buns. I would be behind
the counter with mom and dad. They would smile
whenever those girls came in. Like they were dancing
into the store. "The dance of the soda and candy
purchase"… I just wanted to be them.

OMAR: That's as good a reason to want to do
something…. My dad admired writers. He thought
they were kind of soothsayers.

(A moment passes as CINDY nibbles. OMAR goes to her.)

OMAR: I'll be there for you. More than I have. I won't
ever not have your back again. It's just—sometimes—I
feel like I wouldn't be feeling this constant sense of
fucking up if I hadn't become… *(A laugh of sorts)* if
I hadn't taken that—oath. I know that sounds like
completely stupid. I don't know why I'd feel becoming
a citizen would suddenly turn my world into this place
where success and failure seem like my only options.
But it's like we—bit into this apple. And instead of
getting kicked out into the wilderness, it was the

reverse: we got kicked into the promised land. Where it was all supposed to get better. And I get so mad at myself for disappointing you. Because I did feel I had it in me to make a life for us. In a way that would exceed even my expectations.

CINDY: You never disappointed me. —Not permanently. —Not until last night.

(CINDY *picks up the fork and pokes around in the lasagna again. A moment passes.* OMAR *digests what she just said.*)

CINDY: I don't want to waste this lasagna…. Eat some with me.

(*Slight beat.* OMAR *picks up a fork and joins* CINDY.)

OMAR: Just so you know—you are the real thing. Dancing. I was being unbelievably mean before. You're flat-out amazing, and I'm not just saying that.

CINDY: You are. But thank you.

OMAR: When you first showed me—you blew me away. You just have to dust off those dancing shoes.

CINDY: And a few dead muscles.

OMAR: Sleeping muscles, maybe. Not dead.

CINDY: I certainly wasn't shy that morning. Right there on the street.

(YOUNGER CINDY *and* YOUNGER OMAR *appear again, perhaps downstage now.*)

CINDY: I can't imagine doing that now.

OMAR: But you did do it. You can do it again.

YOUNGER OMAR: Don't think about anything else. Just how you see yourself doing what you most want to do for the rest of your life.

OMAR: You need to imagine that again. You were so— very…

(YOUNGER CINDY performs a dance. It is an accomplished dance. Even masterful. This is clearly a woman with a lot of talent and potential to excel. After a couple of minutes of dancing, she finishes. She is flushed, excited, and smiling. The world is there for the taking. For both of them.)

OMAR: You were so very brilliant.

YOUNGER OMAR: Brilliant.

(YOUNGER OMAR applauds, YOUNGER CINDY takes a bow.)

YOUNGER CINDY: Your turn.

YOUNGER OMAR: What?

YOUNGER CINDY: To dance.

YOUNGER OMAR: Not like that I can't.

YOUNGER CINDY: Like this. *(She holds out her arms inviting him to waltz with her.)* Let's celebrate.

YOUNGER OMAR: Sure. Let's celebrate. *(He moves into her arms.)* Why not.

(Lights fade out on them waltzing around the stage as OMAR and CINDY resume eating. Fade to black)

END OF PLAY

www.ingramcontent.com/pod-product-compliance
Lightning Source LLC
Chambersburg PA
CBHW070023110426
42741CB00034B/2423